MW00990451

Software Requirements
MEMORY JOGGER™

**A Pocket Guide
to Help Software
and Business Teams
Develop and Manage
Requirements**

Ellen Gottesdiener
EBG Consulting, Inc.

First Edition
GOAL/QPC

THE SOFTWARE REQUIREMENTS MEMORY JOGGER™

Ellen Gottesdiener, Author
EBG Consulting, Inc.

Dan Picard, *Project Leader/Editor*
Michele Kierstead, *Cover, Graphic Design, Graphics Production*
Janet MacCausland, *Graphics Production*

GOAL/QPC

8E Industrial Way, Salem, NH 03079
Phone: 800-643-4316 **or** 603-893-1944
Fax: 603-870-9122 **E-mail:** service@goalqpc.com
www.MemoryJogger.org

Printed in the United States of America

First Edition
10 9 8 7 6 5 4 3

ISBN 978-1-57681-060-6

Acknowledgments

Our sincerest thanks to the people and organizations who have contributed their insights, suggestions, and encouragement or who gave us permission to use and adapt their tips, charts, tables, and other information:

Addison-Wesley; Scott Ambler, *Ambysoft Inc.;* T.J. Bogan, *Quality and Compliance Consultant;* James Bossert, *Bank of America;* Susan Burk, *Analysis and Design Coach;* Dr. Al Davis, *University of Colorado at Colorado Springs;* Linda Desmond, PMP, *Project Management Training and Consulting;* Jerry Deville, *Construx Software;* Paul King, *Innovation Technology Services Group, LLC;* Linda Larrivee, *Ultimate Software;* Barbara MacKay, *North Star Facilitators;* Dr. Lawrence D. Pohlmann, *Strategics Consulting;* Bonnie Z. Rapp, *J.P. Morgan Chase;* Richard Rischling, *GE Communications Group;* Sarah Sheard, *Software Productivity Consortium;* Karen Tate, *The Griffin Tate Group;* Steve Tockey, *Construx Software;* Dann Veldkamp, PMP, *Eli Lilly and Company;* Dr. Mark R. Vriesenga, *BAE Systems;* Kathy Walker, *The Center for Systems Management;* and Dr. Karl Wiegers, *Process Impact*

Publisher's Note

Currently, about two-thirds of all software projects undertaken fail to deliver what the customers and users want in a timely, cost-effective way, resulting in billions of dollars lost annually. One of the main reasons that these projects fail is because the teams convened fail to adequately define the software requirements early in the development process. When businesspeople and technical people sit down together to develop new software or to replace existing software, they often find that they have trouble expressing these needs in a way that other team members can understand.

Our goal in creating *The Software Requirements Memory Jogger*™ is to provide a resource that analysts, workshop facilitators, project managers, software developers, and business managers can use to communicate their needs and create a shared understanding when talking about software requirements. This book provides the tools, techniques, and models that team members need to remove barriers to communication and help them achieve their goals. This practical, user-friendly resource is a must for each member of the team and for every employee whose work affects or is affected by the software development process, because it simplifies the process of defining, developing, and managing software requirements. This book will help provide the information that employees and team members need to successfully communicate about and create software that meets the demands of customers and stakeholders.

We believe that the insights and information in this book create a valuable resource that allows teams to attain the highest product quality and reach their performance goals. We hope you will agree.

Dan Picard
Project Leader
GOAL/QPC

How to Use The Software Requirements Memory Jogger™

The Software Requirements Memory Jogger™ is a quick reference guide for you to use on the job or as a supplement to your training. It is designed to facilitate communication between business and technical teams as they define requirements for software projects. It includes the tools, techniques, and models team members will use to elicit, analyze, specify, validate, and manage their software requirements. The book also contains a case study example, set off on a blue background, to show you how to use these tools, techniques, and models in each step of the process.

Not sure what tool, technique, or model to use? Just refer to the User Requirements Model Roadmap in Chapter 4 to direct your efforts. Then refer to the "What Tools and Techniques Will I Use?" chart at the beginning of each chapter to guide you through the process of defining the requirements.

Because many of the terms in this book may not be defined by readers in exactly the same way, we have included a glossary as one of the book's appendices, to ensure that all readers "speak the same language." The terms that are included in the glossary are shown in *blue italics* the first time they appear in the text, to let you know that the term is defined in the back of the book.

You will also find a list of references and resources in the back of the book, in case you want to further your understanding of the tools and concepts in this Memory Jogger™. This list is not meant to be all-inclusive, but it does include the resources that the author felt would be the most helpful to the reader at the time of publication.

We hope that you will find this book to be an invaluable tool that you will use often as you define, develop, and manage your requirements.

What do the different icons mean?

 Alternative names–Sections with this icon will list some of the more-common alternative names that the tools, techniques, models, and documents in this book are known by.

 Key questions–This section will provide some of the questions that you can expect to answer by using this tool, technique, model, or document.

 Links–Sections that include this icon will show you how this model works together with other tools, techniques, and models to help you further define your requirements.

 Tips–When you see sections with this icon, you will get helpful information to assist you in your work with this model.

 Beware!–This icon will alert you to potential pitfalls or problems to watch out for as you use this model.

Contents

Continued on next page

CHAPTER

1

Overview of
Software Requirements

For software to play the vital role it currently performs in our daily lives, software applications must achieve a goal or solve a problem for the *user*.

Requirements are descriptions of the necessary and sufficient properties of a product that will satisfy the consumer's need.

Software requirements, therefore, are descriptions of the necessary and sufficient properties of the *software* that must be met to ensure the product achieves what it was designed to accomplish for its users.

Note: In this book, we will focus on *software requirements* and will use the term *requirements* to refer to these software requirements.

Software applications come in many varieties and may take many forms, such as:

- Business system software – management information systems used within a company to manage operations or core business services (e.g., accounting, payroll, or accounts receivable). (Note: Some organizations satisfy their business systems needs by acquiring *commercial off-the-shelf (COTS)* software developed for an industry-specific market.)

- Embedded software – software, residing in memory, that controls products for consumer and industrial use (e.g., microwaves, dashboard displays, or personal stereos).

- Engineering and scientific software – intensive "number-crunching" software (e.g., orbital dynamics, automated manufacturing, or computer-aided design).

- Expert system software – artificial intelligence computing that solves complex problems (e.g., claim underwriting or Internet searching).

- Personal computing software – software used for personal and business use (e.g., word processing, games, or personal finance).

- Real-time software – software that monitors and analyzes events as they occur, typically within milliseconds (e.g., equipment control and process control).

- System software – software written to service other programs (e.g., file management, operating systems, and compilers).

Systems and system requirements

Many products are referred to as a *system* (i.e., a collection of interrelated elements that work together to achieve an objective). Some products are *complex systems*, composed of interrelated parts or subsystems, each with its own operational capabilities and sets of requirements.

Systems are Composed of Subsystems

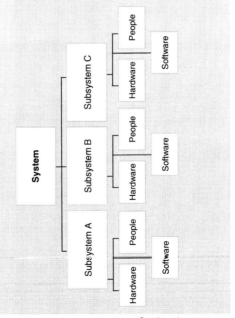

Continued on next page

System requirements define the top-level requirements for *allocation* to subsystems. Each subsystem will, in turn, have its own requirements allocated to *hardware*, *software*, and *people*, which will include requirements for the interfaces among these three components:

- *Hardware* refers to the physical components or devices that have their own set of allocated requirements. Many complex systems have hardware requirements that specify the details for devices (such as memory, power supplies, data storage, physical components and interfaces, and rates of information transfer) that control all of the tangible actions and capabilities that the system's hardware requires.

- The *software* controls the operation of the processing, data, and hardware devices.

- The *people* are the individuals who operate and maintain the system. They may have to satisfy some requirements through manual means. Implementing a system often requires implementing new business practices or changing existing practices, revising job roles and responsibilities, creating and conducting training, documenting and disseminating new job aids, and revising guidelines and procedures. These activities require human action and interaction and, therefore, would need to be allocated to the people who work in the system.

In a system, software requirements describe the software capabilities needed by the system being built, enhanced, or acquired, as well as the constraints on the system's implementation and operation. Requirements, in this book, will refer to the software requirements for any subsystem within a system.

Note: While some of the techniques in this book apply to people interfacing with software, many can be used for hardware interfaces with software as well.

Why should I define requirements?

To deliver a successful software product, you need to develop, document, and validate software requirements. Properly understood requirements allow you to "begin with the end in mind" and are the basis for determining the success of your implemented software. After all, the purpose of software development is to satisfy users' needs, and these needs are precisely what the requirements define.

The price is high for not defining requirements or not doing it well. Poorly defined requirements result in *requirements defects*—errors in requirements caused by incorrect, incomplete, missing, or conflicting requirements. Defective requirements may result in:

- Cost overruns,
- Expensive rework,
- Poor quality,
- Late delivery,
- Dissatisfied *customers*, and
- Exhausted and demoralized team members.

Correcting defective requirements accounts for almost one-half of the cost of software development and is the most expensive kind of development error to fix. Defective requirements become multiplied in number and seriousness as they spread among multiple complex components in design, *code*, and tests. The result is a need for extensive and expensive rework, which costs from ten to one hundred times more to fix later in development.

To reduce the high *risk* of software project failure and the large costs associated with defective requirements, you must properly define requirements early in the software development process.

Requirements verification and validation

Requirements are critical to the success of the end product. Before you write the software's code, the emphasis is on the problem (i.e., defining what to build and ensuring that it is necessary to meet user needs). Although software tests are not executed during *requirements development*, performing conceptual tests will help to uncover incomplete, incorrect, and unclear requirements.

After you have begun to write the code, the emphasis is on testing the software solution against the requirements. Performing *user acceptance tests* will link the original needs back to business customers and end users, ensuring that the right product was built.

As requirements are developed, they are *verified* to see if they satisfy the conditions or specifications of the requirements development activity. *Verification* is like good management—it ensures that you *built the software correctly*.

When requirements are identified and later tested in user acceptance testing, they are *validated* to ensure that they meet user's needs. *Validation* is like good leadership—it ensures that you *built the correct software*.

Whereas *requirements verification* represents the development team's point of view—ensuring the software satisfies the specified requirements, *requirements validation* is concerned with the customer's point of view—ensuring the customer's needs are met.

How Requirements are Verified and Validated

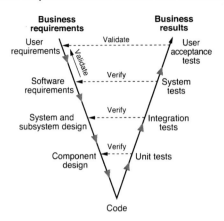

What types of requirements are there?

Software requirements are broadly divided into functional and nonfunctional requirements. *Functional requirements* describe product capabilities—things that the product must do for its users or allow its users to do with the software. Functional requirements are the *doing* part of software—the actions, tasks, and behaviors that users generally interact with. They can be stated as:

- "The system shall provide the capability for schedulers to assign contractors to jobs in their local area."

- "The system shall permit the inventory manager to search for available inventory items."

- "The system shall notify the operator when the temperature exceeds the maximum set value."

- "The system shall store a log of temperature readings every three seconds."

Nonfunctional requirements are properties that the product must have that may not be evident to the user, including quality attributes, constraints, and external interfaces:

- *Quality attributes* describe properties of the software's development and operational environment, such as its performance, capacity, maintainability, portability, reliability, and usability. (See section 5.2 for more information on quality attributes.)

- *Design and implementation constraints* limit how the software can be designed. For example, a limit on the maximum number of concurrent users, the environment that the software will operate in, or a predetermined programming language to be used will all constrain the software design and implementation.

- *External interfaces* are the interfaces with other systems (hardware, software, and human) that the proposed system will interact with.

Nonfunctional requirements are the *being* part of the software—the characteristics and constraints for the software's behavior. They should be documented in quantifiable terms, such as:

- "The response time for loading all estimate information onto the screen shall be no more than six seconds after the user submits the estimate request."

- "During the peak holiday season between November 1st and January 5th, the inventory search capability shall permit 500 simultaneous users to search for inventory items."

- "The system's scheduling capability shall be available weekdays from 7 a.m. PST to 7 p.m. PST."

- "The system shall function on the following operating systems: Isis version 6 or higher and Grok version 2.0 and higher."

Where do requirements come from?

Software requirements operate on three levels: the requirements related to your business, those related to your users, and those that describe the software itself.

Requirements Levels

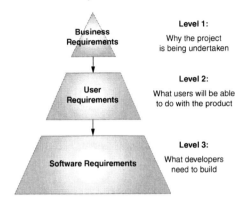

Level 1: Business Requirements

Business requirements are statements of the business rationale for authorizing the project. They include a vision for the software product that is driven by business goals, business objectives, and strategy. Business requirements describe the high-level purpose and needs that the product will satisfy to increase revenue, reduce operating expenses, improve customer service, or meet regulatory obligations. The vision for the product provides a long-term view of what the end product will accomplish for its users and should include a statement of scope to clarify which capabilities the product will and will not provide.

Business requirements can include a high-level description of the software requirements using *features* (i.e., cohesive bundles of externally visible functionality) that align to business goals and objectives. For example, features such as "Provide Payments to Contractors" and "Enable Schedulers to Estimate and Schedule Jobs" should align with one or more business goals such as "Provide Accurate Estimates for Prospective Customers," or with an objective such as "Ninety Percent of All Estimate Requests will result in a Scheduled Job."

Documents that contain business requirements may be referred to as a project charter, vision and scope, business case, marketing requirements, statement of work, document of understanding, product vision, or project scope. A business or software manager is usually the author of the business requirements document and prepares it for an audience that typically includes the project team members, the business team members, and project *sponsors*.

Business Purpose for the ClearVisual Glass Cleaners (CVGC) Case Study

ClearVisual is a Web-based software application that will provide estimating, scheduling, billing, contractor (i.e., glass cleaner) payments, and marketing capabilities for window-cleaning companies. Multiple cleaning companies across the country will subscribe to the service and maintain all of their company data on ClearVisual software.

Level 2: User Requirements

User requirements are the definition of the software requirements from the user's point of view. They describe the tasks that users need to accomplish with the software and the necessary quality characteristics of the software. (Users can be broadly defined to include not only humans who access the software but hardware devices and other software systems as well.)

Documents that contain user requirements are often called operational capabilities, product features, concept of operations, or *use cases*. Although some organizations do not create a separate *user requirements document*, those that do usually have an *analyst* write the user requirements document. While users are the primary audience for the user requirements, technical staff can also benefit from understanding user needs and should review user requirements.

User requirements are the bridge between the business goals (expressed in business language) and the detailed software requirements (expressed in more-technical language). For this reason, it is important to ensure that the analysts who write the requirements have excellent communication skills, as well as knowledge of user *requirements models* (described in Chapter 4 of this book).

Level 3: Software Requirements

Software requirements are detailed descriptions of all of the functional and nonfunctional requirements that the software must fulfill to meet business and user needs, while staying within the limits of the known design and implementation constraints. Software requirements establish an agreement between technical people and businesspeople on what the product must do.

Names for documents that contain software requirements include the *software requirements specification*, detailed requirements, specification, technical specification, or functional specification. Typically, the authors of the software requirements specification are analysts, and the primary audience for the software requirements are the software *providers*—the developers, testers, and others who will provide the software. However, business customers should also review and approve the software requirements. (Both business and software provider audiences are possible in organizations where one document combines both user and software requirements.)

How should I document my requirements?

There are a few ways to represent requirements information.

You can represent requirements as textual statements organized as an outline:

Requirements as a Text Outline

FR 1.0: Job Scheduling
    FR 1.1: Locate Schedule Slot
    FR 1.2: Find Available Contractors
        etc.
FR 2.0: Maintain Contractors
        etc.

(Note: FR = Functional Requirements)

Tip

Textual requirements statements are often depicted as a tree diagram, with each requirement statement decomposed to its lowest level of detail to create a text hierarchy.

Requirements as a Tree Diagram

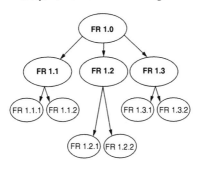

You can also represent requirements as user requirements models (i.e., diagrams, tables, or text) that represent information visually or in natural language. These models are explained in detail in the subsequent chapters of this book.

Requirements as Models

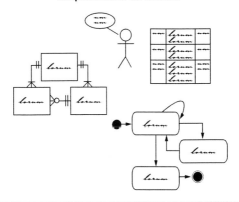

Good requirements documentation practices

As you use the user requirements models in this book to document your requirements, be sure to follow "good requirements documentation practices" to ensure a successful requirements development process:

- Define your business requirements using textual statements, then supplement the definition of the product scope with one or more diagrams. (See Chapters 2 and 4 for help in defining the project scope.)

- Represent your user requirements with a variety of models such as use cases, *actors*, and other representations. (These models will be explained in Chapter 4.) This makes the requirements definition process more interesting and appealing, and allows users to express requirements in different, yet related, ways. Using multiple models will also increase the quality of software by revealing missing and erroneous requirements.

- Supplement outline forms of text software requirements (see Chapter 5) with user requirements models.

What are the characteristics of excellent requirements?

Gathering and documenting high-quality requirements is critical to successful product development and acceptance. To ensure that you are developing excellent requirements, make sure that all of your requirements are:

- **Correct**: They accurately represent the real needs of users and *stakeholders*.

- **Complete**: They include all of the needed elements—functionality, external interfaces, quality attributes, and design constraints.

- **Clear**: They can be understood in the same way by all stakeholders with minimal supplementary explanation.
- **Concise**: They are stated simply in the minimal possible way to be understandable.
- **Consistent**: They do not conflict with other requirements.
- **Relevant**: They are necessary to meet a business need, goal, or objective.
- **Feasible**: They are possible to implement.
- **Verifiable**: There is a finite, cost-effective technique for determining whether the requirement is satisfied.

Key practices that promote excellent requirements

- Develop a clear vision for the end product.
- Develop a well-defined, shared understanding of the project scope.
- Involve stakeholders throughout the requirements process.
- Represent and discover requirements using multiple models.
- Document the requirements clearly and consistently.
- Continually validate that the requirements are the right ones to focus on.
- Verify the quality of the requirements early and frequently.
- Prioritize the requirements and remove unnecessary ones.

Continued on next page

- Establish a *baseline* for requirements (i.e., a "snapshot in time" of the reviewed and agreed-upon requirements that will serve as a basis for further development).
- Trace the requirements' origins and how they link to other requirement and system elements.
- Anticipate and manage any requirements changes.

What is requirements engineering?

Requirements engineering—a discipline within systems and software engineering that encompasses all of the activities and deliverables associated with defining a product's requirements—is one of the best ways to develop excellent requirements. Requirements engineering is comprised of requirements development and *requirements management*.

Requirements Development and Requirements Management

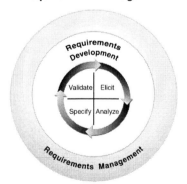

Requirements development involves activities that *Elicit*, *Analyze*, *Specify*, and *Validate* the requirements:

- Elicit: Identify the stakeholders, documentation, and external sources of requirements information, and solicit requirements from those sources.

- Analyze: Define the product scope and user goals, explore how users will interact with the system, and develop user requirements models to study and communicate requirements to business and technical audiences. Verify the requirements to identify inconsistencies, ambiguities, omissions, and errors, and allocate requirements to the software. Prioritize the requirements by removing unnecessary ones and ranking the rest to make implementation decisions.

- Specify: Differentiate and document functional and nonfunctional requirements, identify important requirements quality attributes and constraints, and check that the requirements are documented unambiguously and completely.

- Validate: Examine the requirements to ensure that they satisfy the customer needs.

  Note: Requirements development is a progressively elaborating, or iterative, process—requirements are developed by starting with a small set of requirements and increasingly adding details.

Requirements management activities support and control the requirements information defined during requirements development. Requirements management involves activities that:

- *Establish a baseline* by documenting the current state of requirements at a point in time, to use as a starting point. The baseline shows a set of requirements with an agreed-upon status at a particular point in time and captures important attributes about the requirements. Developing a baseline creates a reference to use to track how requirements evolve over time.

- *Control change* by establishing mechanisms and policies for recognizing, evaluating, and deciding how to integrate new and evolving requirements into an existing requirements baseline.

- *Trace requirements* by identifying and documenting how requirements are logically related, and identifying the lineage of each requirement. *Requirements traceability* allows you to identify how the requirements link to business goals and objectives (backward tracing or requirements derivation) and to future development deliverables (forward tracing).

The requirements development and requirements management processes (along with the need to "set the stage" for these processes) involve many activities and can be decomposed into numerous substeps, as shown on the next page.

Requirements Development and Management Activities

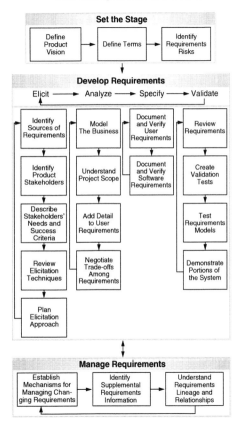

Set the Stage

| Define Product Vision | → | Define Terms | → | Identify Requirements Risks |

Develop Requirements

Elicit → Analyze → Specify → Validate

Identify Sources of Requirements	Model The Business	Document and Verify User Requirements	Review Requirements
Identify Product Stakeholders	Understand Project Scope	Document and Verify Software Requirements	Create Validation Tests
Describe Stakeholders' Needs and Success Criteria	Add Detail to User Requirements		Test Requirements Models
Review Elicitation Techniques	Negotiate Trade-offs Among Requirements		Demonstrate Portions of the System
Plan Elicitation Approach			

Manage Requirements

| Establish Mechanisms for Managing Changing Requirements | → | Identify Supplemental Requirements Information | → | Understand Requirements Lineage and Relationships |

The applicable outputs for requirements development and management are described in the following table:

Activity	Outputs	Described in Chapter:
Setting the Stage	• Product vision • Glossary • Requirements risk mitigation strategy	2
Elicit	• Requirements sources list • Stakeholder categories and stakeholder profiles • Stakeholder elicitation plan	3
Analyze	• Business models (as applicable) • Scope-level requirements • Detailed user requirements • Prioritized requirements	4
Specify	• User requirements document (as needed) • Software requirements specification	5
Validate	• Validated requirements	6
Manage Requirements	• Requirements baseline • Requirements attributes • Change control process and requirements trace matrices	7
Adapt Requirements Practices	• Tailored requirements development and management practices • Lessons learned about what requirements practices worked and what should be changed	8

Why is it important to let requirements evolve?

Understanding of requirements increases throughout requirements development. Once software development begins, the cost of changes in requirements increases dramatically. For these reasons, it is important to develop requirements in a manner that accelerates requirements understanding while producing them as thoroughly as possible for the scope of software development.

An effective way to accomplish this is to develop requirements in an iterative manner. To develop requirements iteratively:

- Use *elicitation* techniques that allow customers to validate their requirements as early in the elicitation process as possible. These techniques include *prototyping, facilitated workshops*, and user task analysis. (See Chapter 3 for more information on these techniques.)

- Develop requirements using multiple short cycles or *iterations*. Each cycle or iteration is a self-contained period of time with a set of activities—elicitation, analysis, specification, and validation. Each iteration results in a subset of requirements that you will use as a basis for further requirements development.

- Conduct short *requirements retrospectives* at the end of each *requirements iteration* to learn and improve your requirements process. (A *retrospective* is a special meeting where the team explores what works, what doesn't work, what could be learned from the just-completed iteration, and how to adapt processes and techniques before starting the next iteration. Chapter 8 explains requirements retrospectives in more detail.)

Who is involved?

Requirements development and requirements management involves many stakeholders in numerous roles. The typical software project begins with a sponsor, who approves the rationale for the project and thereby authorizes the product development effort. Responsibility then shifts to the project manager, subject matters experts, and analysts. In large organizations, the role of the analyst is to develop and manage requirements documentation as subject matter experts define the requirements. Software developers and testers are the requirements consumers who use the requirements to design, build, install, and test the application.

Project Sponsor

- Allocates resources (people, materials, and funding) for the project
- Ensures that project goals and objectives align with organizational aims
- Marshals appropriate participation (by customers and users) in the project
- Defines or approves the overall vision and scope for the product
- Makes decisions about the scope of the project and product release issues
- Resolves conflicts in requirements priorities
- May delegate authority for approving detailed requirements to business experts or business management

Project or Product Manager

- Acts as a liaison between the software team and the business management or product development organization
- Coordinates user involvement
- Ensures that the analysts and subject matter experts have the needed resources, tools, training, and knowledge to develop requirements and manage the requirements process
- Institutes the requirements change control process
- Oversees requirements prioritization
- Monitors the progress of requirements development and management

---

Analyst

- Selects elicitation techniques and coordinates or facilitates the elicitation activities
- Collaborates with business experts and users to develop requirements
- Coordinates requirements management activities
- Drafts models and documents
- Translates user requirements into specifications
- Monitors changing requirements and coordinates negotiation
- Verifies that requirements are necessary, correct, complete, and consistent

Note: Some organizations may refer to an analyst as a system engineer, requirements engineer, or business analyst. When developing requirements for complex systems, an analyst also defines requirements for interfacing subsystems and technical components of the overall system.

Subject Matter Expert

- Provides details about user needs (and may, in fact, be a user)
- Provides details about the business processes, rules, and data
- Identifies additional people who can advise on the requirements
- Represents the needs of users who cannot be directly involved in requirements development
- Identifies and consults with other subject matter experts or *advisors* who have relevant requirements knowledge
- Ensures that requirements align with the product vision

- Reviews requirements documentation to ensure that it adequately and completely represents user needs
- Participates in creating or reviewing requirements models and documents
- Prioritizes requirements

Note: For COTS and other commercial software, marketing or product development staff may act as subject matter experts, representing the user community in requirements development. Marketing or product development staff may also serve as analysts.

Software Developer and Tester

- Provides details about design constraints and suggestions regarding the feasibility of nonfunctional requirements
- May contribute to writing portions of the software requirements specification
- Reviews all requirements documentation
- Reviews software specifications to ensure that they can be transformed into a feasible software design
- Ensures that the requirements can be tested

Defining requirements is largely a process of discovery, so the people involved (i.e., analysts and business experts) should have a high tolerance for uncertainty during the process, as well as a strong need for clarity and closure.

Key Project Roles and What They Do

| | Requirements Development | | | Requirements Management |
	Define business requirements	Develop user requirements	Specify software requirements	
Project Sponsor	Owner, Approver	Reviewer	Approver	Approver
Project or Product Manager	Producer	Reviewer	Reviewer	Reviewer
Analyst	Reviewer	Producer	Producer	Producer
Subject Matter Expert	Reviewer	Owner, Approver, Producer	Owner, Reviewer	Owner
Software Developer and Tester	Reviewer	Reviewer	Reviewer, Producer (possibly)	Reviewer

Table Key:
Owner: Provides correct and complete information; provides requirements change notification
Approver: Approves and authorizes requirements
Producer: Creates and maintains requirements
Reviewer: Stays informed; provides information and feedback

What is management's role?

Business and software managers need to ensure that the team develops excellent requirements and manages them appropriately. To promote an environment that ensures the development of good requirements practices, managers should:

- Ensure a project sponsor is clearly identified.
- Ensure the product vision and scope are defined early and unambiguously.
- Ensure that the right stakeholders will be involved in requirements development, including knowledgeable business experts and people who accurately represent user needs.
- Ensure that the team uses good requirements practices to develop excellent requirements.
- Resolve requirements prioritization conflicts, or assign an appropriate decision maker to do so.
- Ensure the team has the training, education, and knowledge to develop and manage requirements.
- Monitor requirements progress and remove barriers for the team.

CHAPTER
2

Setting the Stage
for Requirements Development

Before you can develop the right software requirements, you need to perform certain activities to establish a shared understanding of the product and its stakeholders, to "set the stage" for effective software development.

To create this shared understanding and facilitate the requirements development process, you need to define a common vision for the product among the stakeholders, and clarify the meaning of important product-related terms. You will also need to establish a strategy for identifying and dealing with any requirements-related risks that you may encounter.

What Tools and Techniques Will I Use to Set the Stage?

When you need to:	Then create:
Define the product vision	A Vision Statement
Clarify terms	A Glossary
Identify requirements risks	A Requirements Risk Mitigation Strategy

2.1 Vision Statement

What is it?

The *vision statement* is a concise statement that defines the what, why, and who of the end software product from a business point of view. It serves as an "elevator test"—something that you can explain in a minute or so, as if to someone between floors in an elevator. The vision statement can be included in another document (such as the product charter, project initiation, or project vision document) that establishes a business case, overall business goals, objectives, and other information related to how the project will operate.

Alternative names for this tool

- Product Differentiation Statement
- Product Position Statement

Why use it?

To define a common understanding of the final software product.

What does it do?

- Ensures that the product definition aligns with business goals and objectives
- Broadly identifies product stakeholders
- Describes the state of the business and how the world of users will be different after the project is successfully completed
- Provides team members with a simple, easy-to-reference description of the project

Key questions that this tool will answer

- Who will buy or use this product?
- What will the product do for its stakeholders?
- What are the reasons to buy or use this product?
- What will the state of the business or operational environment be once this product is available?
- How will it be distinguished in the marketplace?

How do I do it?

1. **Define the following terms:**

   - Target customers: Describe the people who will use or buy the software.
   - Statement of need or opportunity: Describe what the target customers do, and explain how this product will help them do it.
   - Product name: Provide the name of the product that you will create.
   - Product category: Describe the type of product that you are building. Product categories might include internal business software application, COTS software, embedded software, game software, hardware device, or complex system.
   - Key benefit or compelling reason to buy: Describe what the product will do for the target customers or the justification for buying the product.
   - Primary competitive alternative, current system, or current manual process: Describe the key competing products available or the system or process that the product will replace.
   - Statement of primary product differentiation: Explain the differences between the product you are building and the competition.

2. **Create the vision statement by inserting the defined terms into a template as follows:**

   For <target customers> **who** <statement of the need or opportunity>, **the** <product name> **is a** <product category> **that** <key benefit or compelling reason to buy>.

   Unlike <primary competitive alternative, current system, or current manual process>, **our product** <statement of primary product differentiation>. *[Reference 1: Moore, 1999]*

3. **Review the vision statement and check to see that it aligns with your organization's business goals and objectives.**

   - Have the sponsor ensure that the vision fits with departmental and organizational goals and objectives.
   - Have team members, ideally in collaboration with the project sponsor, review and revise the vision statement as needed.

 CVGC Vision Statement

For service companies and their staff **who** provide window-cleaning services to homes and commercial sites, **the** CVGC system **is a** Web-based software application **that** estimates and schedules jobs, assigns staff to jobs, promotes company services, and retains current customers. **Unlike** existing products that don't allow multiple companies to collaborate on bids or optimize staff assignments to jobs, **our product** allows multiple companies to use the application, provides full life-cycle business services for the entire operation (including accounts payable and receivables), and is easy to use.

Variations

2.1.1 Problem Statement

A *problem statement* describes a current problem that the business is experiencing and clarifies what a successful solution would look like. A problem statement is useful when the solution involves enhancing existing software or when product implementation creates a need for a business process change. It can also help you to begin to define the product vision.

Use the following template to create a problem statement:

> **The problem of** <insert statement of problem> **affects** <name affected people, organizations, or customer groups>. **The impact of this is** <name the impact (i.e., poor decisions, cost overruns, erroneous information or processes, slow response time to customers, etc.)>. **A successful solution would** <describe the solution>.

 CVGC Problem Statement

The problem of quoting and scheduling jobs and paying contractors using the current manual and automated process **affects** customers, contractors, schedulers, and bookkeepers. **The impact of this is** inaccurate estimates, double-booking of contractors, empty spaces in our job schedule, and over- or underpayment of contractors. **A successful solution would** allow immediate answers to quote requests using contractors working in the customer's postal code, provide the ability to schedule and complete jobs within one week of request, enable prompt customer invoicing, and issue weekly contractor payments.

Links to other tools

- Targeted customers in the vision statement can become users in the stakeholder categories. (See section 3.2 for more information on stakeholder categories.)

- Targeted customers can become actors in the *actor table*. (See section 4.6 for more information on actor tables.)

2.2 Glossary

What is it?

A *glossary* is a dictionary of common terms relevant to the product being built, enhanced, or acquired. You will use the terms in the glossary during requirements elicitation, in requirements documentation, and throughout the project.

Alternative names for this tool

- Business Glossary
- Concepts Catalog

Why use it?

To establish a common vocabulary for key business terms and to help team members reach a mutual understanding of those terms. Different stakeholders may use the same term to mean different things or different terms to mean the same thing, causing confusion and expending valuable energy in communicating about requirements.

What does it do?

- Provides a shared understanding of the problem domain

- Enables businesspeople to inform technical people about important business concepts

- Provides a foundation for defining requirements models such as *business rules*, *data models*, and use cases

- Saves time and effort during requirements development by eliminating misunderstandings in what business concepts really mean

 ### Key questions that this tool will answer

- What do the terms and business concepts that we use mean?

How do I do it?

1. **Determine who on the project can best identify a starting list of terms.**

   - Include subject matter experts.

   - Include data analysts from the software development organization (who are often adept at defining business terms).

2. **Identify important terms relevant to the business domain.**

   - Examine the nouns in any existing project documents (e.g., the project charter, product vision statement, and problem statement).

   - Include terms related to:

     - Businesses and business parties (e.g., clients, customers, prospects, vendors, providers, distributors, and service providers).

     - Places and locations (e.g., addresses and sites).

     - Events (e.g., jobs, work orders, requests, shipments, and production).

     - Agreements (e.g., contracts, estimates, and discounts).

- Accounts (e.g., customer accounts, financial records, and balances).

- Products and services (e.g., employee services and materials and goods).

- Markets and prospects (e.g., business parties, providers, contractors, customers, vendors, and distributors).

- Resources (e.g., buildings, assets, machines, devices, contractors, employees, and schedules)

• Review any existing business processes or systems documentation for terms and their definitions.

3. **Draft definitions for the terms.**

• Orient each definition to readers who have no business experience or knowledge about the term.

• Add "aliases" or alternative names when multiple terms have the same meaning.

• Include commonly used acronyms after each term, where applicable.

• Add examples for clarification when helpful. For example, use qualifiers (such as "prospective customer" instead of "customer") in terms to help with clarification.

• Ask one person to draft a definition of each term.

4. **Identify multiple stakeholders to review the definitions and revise the definitions as needed to arrive at an agreement for each term.**

 You can also create a separate project glossary section for project terms (such as project roles, organization names, software methods, and tools).

Software Requirements

Tip Because you should expect the glossary to evolve as the team iterates through requirements, you may want to appoint a "glossary guardian"— someone in charge of keeping the glossary up-to-date and used consistently in all requirements models and requirements discussions. Ideally, this would be a businessperson; otherwise, an analyst is a good candidate for this role.

CVGC Glossary

Term	Definition	Aliases	Examples
Job	A set of services provided to a customer at a specific site on a specific day	• Work order	• Clean 25 pane windows, 3 inside mirrors, and 1 skylight at 49 Pyle Drive.
Contractor	A business entity (usually one or more persons) performing the work	• Sub-contractor • Worker	• Jeff Rhodes • Avion Glen
Site	Physical locations with one or more addresses associated with one customer. Can be residential or commercial, and may or may not be occupied by the customer. (Jobs are performed at sites.)	• Job site • Job location	• 123 Corporate Way, Anytown, USA

⊂∞⊃ *Links to other models*

- Terms in the glossary will appear in:
  - *Relationship maps* and *process maps* as nouns on flows.
  - *Context diagrams* as nouns on flows (both in and out of the system) or as external entities.
  - Data models as entities and attributes.
  - States in *state diagrams*.
  - Use case names and use case steps.
  - Business rules.

2.3   Requirements Risk Mitigation Strategy

What is it?

The *requirements risk mitigation strategy* assesses requirements-related risks and identifies actions to avoid or minimize those risks. Requirements risks are requirements-related occurrences or conditions that could endanger your project or your development of a successful product. Risks should be evaluated, tracked and controlled throughout the project.

Note: Risk management is a large project-management topic and this section addresses only requirements-related risks. While some product-level risks can be positive (such as high demand for the product), the focus here is on negative circumstances surrounding requirements development and management.

 Alternative names for this tool

- Requirements Risk Management Plan
- Requirements Risk Assessment Plan

Why use it?

To strengthen team and customer communication and to help the project team prepare for or prevent obstacles to successful requirements development and management. Because requirements are so critical to the project, identifying and addressing requirements risks can have a big impact on your success.

What does it do?

- Identifies risks that might prevent the effective development and management of requirements
- Involves multiple project stakeholders in ranking each requirements risk according to its likelihood of occurring and its potential impact
- Allows the team to communicate openly and honestly about potential obstacles
- Identifies ways for the team to proactively manage risks

Key questions that this tool will answer

- What risks do we face in defining requirements?
- How can we mitigate the most severe risks?

How do I do it?

1. **Assemble stakeholders to review and tailor a list of potential requirements risks.**

   - Use a starter list of common requirements risks, such as:
     - Lack of user involvement.
     - Unrealistic customer expectations.
     - Developers adding unnecessary functionality.
     - Constantly changing requirements (i.e., requirements creep).

- Poor impact analysis when requirements change and evolve.

- Use of new requirements techniques or tools.

- Unclear, ambiguous requirements.

- Conflicting requirements.

- Missing requirements.

• Brainstorm additional risks based on the prior experience of the team. Be sure to include risks that could be caused by company culture and environment.

 Tip

To help identify possible risks, ask, "What events or conditions could cause problems during requirements development or slow us down?"

2. **Rank the risks.**

• Analyze each risk according to its probability and impact.

- *Probability* is an estimate of how likely it is that the risk will cause a problem. Use a scale or range such as:

  a) Low = Remote to small chance (0%–25% chance) that the risk will be realized.

  b) Medium = Moderate probability (26%–74% chance) of the risk occurring.

  c) High = Great probability or certainty (75%–100% chance) that the risk will occur.

- *Impact* is the degree to which the risk will negatively affect the requirements process. Use a scale such as:

  a) Low = Negligible; may present some impact.

  b) Medium = Manageable or marginal impact.

  c) High = Critical or catastrophic impact; major problems will need to be addressed.

- Rank each risk along each dimension (probability and impact).

 Be sure that everyone understands the ranking scheme. Stakeholders may have differing opinions about how to rank probability and impact. Allow stakeholders to discuss and clarify any differing opinions about their rankings and strive to reach consensus on ranking each requirements risk.

3. **Plot the final rankings and agree on which risks you will address after they have been ranked.**

   - One way to plot the final rankings might be:

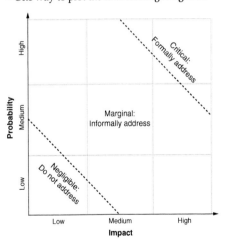

4. **Identify ways to control, avoid, or mitigate any critical risks.**

   - Assign each critical risk to a team member who will take responsibility for monitoring that risk. Identify the actions he or she will take, the resources needed to carry out the actions, and the way he or she will communicate the actions to the team.

- Ensure that sponsors and team leaders agree to the actions.
- Make sure that team members understand how their actions affect their requirements work.
- Monitor the risks throughout requirements development and management.
- Analyze and add new requirements risks as they occur, and update the risk mitigation strategy as needed.

Common Requirements Risk	Risk Mitigation Strategies	For More Information, See Chapter:
Lack of user involvement	· Identify product stakeholders	3
	· Create a stakeholder involvement plan	3
	· Use elicitation techniques (such as exploratory prototypes and requirements workshops) that entice users into the process	3
Unrealistic customer expectations	· Create a product vision	2
	· Develop project scope models	4
	· Validate requirements with operational prototypes	6
Developers adding unnecesary functionality	· Create a product vision	2
	· Prioritize requirements	4
Constantly changing requirements (requirements creep)	· Develop scope models	4
	· Create a baseline for requirements and establish change control mechanisms	7
Poor impact analysis when requirements change and evolve	· Create a baseline and trace requirements	7
	· Formally document the requirements	5

Continued on next page

Common Requirements Risk	Risk Mitigation Strategies	For More Information, See Chapter:
Use of new requirements techniques or tools	• Adapt the requirements process for the project	8
	• Conduct ongoing requirements retrospectives	8
Unclear, ambiguous requirements	• Develop a product vision	2
	• Develop multiple requirements models	4
	• Validate the requirements with model validation, acceptance tests, and peer reviews	6
Conflicting requirements	• Formally document the requirements	5
	• Validate the requirements with model validation and inspections and reviews	6
Missing requirements	• Develop multiple requirements models	4
	• Verify requirements for missing requirements with model validation using walk-throughs and with peer reviews	6

Common Risk Mitigation Strategies

Note: Many risk mitigation actions involve establishing and following good requirements management practices. On smaller projects, you can manage risks informally as long the team reviews the risks periodically.

Make sure that *all* of the critical requirements risks have an owner who is responsible for implementing mitigation actions. Educate the owner about the risk so he or she can take responsibility for the necessary mitigation actions. (A project sponsor, who may not even be aware of the risk, can own some requirements risks.)

Completing a form or checklist alone does not control risks. Make sure that you implement the mitigation actions and monitor the risks. Check periodically to see if the actions are working and if new risks are emerging, and make adjustments as needed.

CVGC Requirements Risk Mitigation Strategy

Risk Factor	Probability of Risk	Impact of Risk	Risk Mitigation Strategy	Team Member Responsible
Unavailability of the CVGC company owner to clarify scope	Medium	High	• Conduct a visioning workshop with the owner present and create scope models in the workshop. • Preschedule a biweekly review meeting.	Trisha Faith
No involvement from contractors	Medium	High	• Conduct a "shadow" visit (i.e., follow a contractor to a job site for a half day). • Conduct interviews with 8 random contractors. • Hold a half-day workshop with 3 contractors to create related requirements models. (Andy will compensate their time by paying for one job.) • Conduct 2 paper prototype walk-throughs with 3 candidate contractors at their home office during the requirements gathering process.	Adam Reese

CHAPTER
3
Elicit
the Requirements

One of the most crucial and challenging aspects of software development is defining the requirements for the proposed software. Elicitation identifies the sources for these requirements and then evokes the requirements from those sources. Requirements elicitation is a "human-intensive" activity that relies on the involvement of stakeholders as a primary source of the needed requirements.

Requirement elicitation is primarily the responsibility of the analyst, but it can involve other technical staff who benefit from acquiring a deeper understanding of stakeholder needs by being involved.

Why is it difficult to elicit requirements?

Customers and users often do not understand how software design and development works, and cannot specify their own software requirements in a way that works for developers. For their part, software developers often do not understand the problems and needs of customers and users well enough to specify the requirements on their behalf.

Continued on next page

Typical difficulties include:

- Differing and sometimes conflicting needs among different types of users.
- Unstated or assumed requirements on the part of stakeholders.
- Gaining access to knowledgeable stakeholders.
- An inability to envision new or different ways to use software.
- Uncertainty about how to adapt to changing business needs.
- Having a large number of highly interrelated requirements.
- Having limited time to elicit requirements from busy stakeholders.
- Overcoming resistance to change.

To help you overcome these many difficulties, you must encourage an environment of cooperation and communication among the developers, customers, and users, to ensure that you elicit the appropriate requirements.

How do I elicit software requirements?

To effectively elicit requirements, you will need to:

1. **Select and plan your requirements elicitation techniques.**

   - Identify the sources for your requirements.
   - Be sure that you thoroughly understand your stakeholders and the best way to involve them in requirements elicitation by creating a stakeholder elicitation plan. (See section 3.12 for more information on stakeholder elicitation plans.)
   - Choose a combination of elicitation techniques.

- Estimate how long using each technique will take, generate a list of planned tasks, and allocate people to accomplish those tasks. (Be cognizant of scheduling difficulties that might arise if you plan to elicit requirements from people who are located at a distant location from the analysts who are eliciting the requirements.)

- Plan on multiple iterations through requirements elicitation to ensure that requirements evolve.

2. **Set goals and expectations and prepare.**

- Determine the desired outcome for each technique (e.g., to obtain initial requirements for determining the project scope or to explore the requirements of a particular user group).

- Prepare the tools and techniques (e.g., an agenda, interview questions, list of existing documents, or people to contact) that will make your elicitation more effective and efficient.

- Notify the stakeholders you will use for each elicitation activity and allow them time to prepare for the activity. Provide useful information (such as an agenda or the interview questions) in advance to set the context for the elicitation technique you will use.

- Arrange for logistics (e.g., location, food, materials, etc.), as needed.

3. **Elicit the requirements.**

- Use the techniques described in this chapter to determine exactly what your stakeholders' requirements are.

- Document the information you collect during the elicitation process, to reduce errors or missing information.

- Respect stakeholders' time when using techniques that involve direct stakeholder interaction. Start and end on time when interviewing stakeholders, observing users, conducting user task analysis, or facilitating workshops and *focus groups*.

4. **Verify and correct your findings.**

- Share the documentation with all of your team members. Conduct *peer reviews* of the documentation to ensure the documented requirements accurately describe user needs. (See section 6.1 for more information on conducting peer reviews.)

- Revise the documentation based on feedback from the stakeholders.

5. **Repeat steps 1-4 to deepen the team's understanding of requirements.**

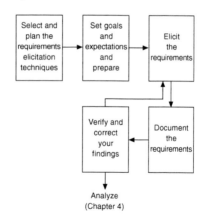

What Tools and Techniques Will I Use to Elicit Requirements?

When you need to:	Then create:
Identify sources of requirements	A Requirements Source List
Identify product stakeholders	Stakeholder Categories
Describe stakeholders' needs and success criteria	Stakeholder Profiles
Review elicitation techniques	Identified Combinations of Elicitation Techniques: Interviews, Exploratory Prototypes, Facilitated Workshops, Focus Groups, User Task Analysis, Observation, Existing Documentation Study
Plan an elicitation approach	A Stakeholder Elicitation Plan

3.1 Requirements Source List

What is it?

The requirements source list is an inventory of the people, specific documents, and external information sources that you will elicit requirements from.

Why do it?

To identify potential documentation sources of requirements and allow analysts to elicit, review, document, and verify requirements information with stakeholders.

What does it do?

- Identifies sources of requirements information
- Facilitates planning for efficiently involving stake-holders

How do I do it?

1. **Identify the relevant stakeholders that you should elicit requirements from.**

   - Be sure to consider *all* of the project stakeholders. Include the customers who sponsor and champion the software development, the users who will interact directly or indirectly with the software, and others who have knowledge or a stake in the product.

   - Develop a stakeholder elicitation plan for each stakeholder. (See section 3.12 for more information on developing a stakeholder elicitation plan.) Keep in mind that stakeholders are often busy and need advance notice to participate in requirements elicitation.

2. **Identify any documentation that you can use as a source of requirements information.**

   - Include physically accessible references from prior manual and automated systems, such as:
     - Existing and interfacing systems documentation.
     - Change requests, software *defect* lists, customer complaint logs, and issues lists.
     - User guides, training materials, and work procedures guidelines.
     - Help desk documentation.
     - Policies and procedure guides.
     - Code in existing systems.

---

3. **Identify external sources of information.**
   - Include:
     - Departments or service companies that provide market survey data and industry analysis.
     - Descriptions and reviews of competitive software products and product materials.
     - Sales, marketing, and communication materials.
     - Regulations, guidelines, and laws from governmental agencies and regulatory bodies.

3.2 Stakeholder Categories

What are they?

Stakeholder categories are structured arrangements of groups or individuals who have a vested interest in the software product you are developing.

Alternative names for this tool
- Stakeholder Classes
- Stakeholder Statement

Why do it?

To understand who has an interest in or influence on the project, who will use the software and its outputs, and who the product will affect in some way. (These groups and individuals will need to be kept informed about progress, conflicts, changes, and priorities in requirements information.)

What does it do?

- Specifies the types of people who have requirements and need to be involved or represented in the requirements elicitation process
- Distinguishes the product's customers from its users
- Clarifies which people and external agencies you should consult

- Encourages the team to consider involving often-overlooked people

Incomplete understanding of stakeholders can result in missing or erroneous requirements or developing the wrong software solution. Be sure that you understand and include *all* of your stakeholders before proceeding to software development.

Key questions that this tool will answer

- Who affects or is affected by the system?
- Who or what interacts with the system?
- Who has knowledge relevant to the requirements?

What are the categories of stakeholders?

There are three categories of stakeholders: customers, users, and other stakeholders.

Stakeholder Categories

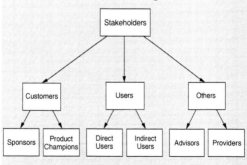

Continued on next page

Customers are responsible for accepting or paying for the software product. Subcategories of customer stakeholders include:

- *Sponsors*, who authorize or legitimize the product development effort by contracting or paying for the project. (Sponsors may also be called backers, buyers, guarantors, owners, or benefactors.)

Sponsor influence is sometimes necessary to obtain appropriate stakeholder involvement. Be sure to review the list of stakeholders with the sponsor to keep him or her informed about relevant stakeholders.

- *Product champions*, who ensure that the software meets the needs of multiple user communities. Product champions identify the users who should participate in requirements development to ensure that the right requirements are gathered. Product champions can themselves be the end users of the product, and your product may have multiple champions if you have multiple types of *direct users*. (Product champions are also called ambassador users, publicists, and product visionaries.)

Consider where the product will be used to help you identify customers:

- With software developed for internal use, internal customers may include executives and management who want to gain business benefit from the project through business process improvements, increased safety, efficiency, customer satisfaction, or sales.

- With software developed for external use, external customers may include a manager in a company authorizing a

Continued on next page

COTS software acquisition, a governmental agency contracting the development of a complex product, a small business owner buying accounting software, or a venture capitalist funding a software vendor's new product. These customers will benefit by purchasing the software as a ready-made or custom solution, rather than building it themselves. (**Note**: When you have a large number of diverse acquiring customers, people within the developing organization (e.g., people from marketing, product development, or procurement) can act as *surrogates* (i.e., stand-ins or substitutes who take the place of stakeholders) for external customers.)

Users come into contact with the software product or are affected by it in some way. User subcategories include:

- *Direct users*, who are the parties (i.e., people, organizations, system components, or devices) that directly interact with the software (e.g., a person who requests information from the system through a user interface, a system that sends or receives data files, or a device that sends or receives signals or messages).

- *Indirect users*, who do not directly interact with the system but can come into contact with system products (e.g., reports, invoices, databases, and other tangible assets) generated by the system. (Indirect users also include people who may be affected by the decisions or actions made as a result of system outputs.)

Continued on next page

Other stakeholders have knowledge about the product or an interest in its development and maintenance. Subcategories for other stakeholders include:

- *Advisors*, who have relevant information about the software product. Advisors can include subject matter experts, operational support staff, product development and marketing staff, system administrators, data administrators, legal staff, regulatory agencies, auditors, trainers, human resource staff, and performance improvement staff.

Advisors often know the vital business rules that must be incorporated into the software product, even if they do not directly interact with the product itself. Missing the requirements that deal with business rules can result in costly rework. Be sure that you identify the advisors for your project and involve them in your requirements elicitation process.

- *Providers*, who design and produce the software by transforming the requirements into the final product. Providers include project team members (such as analysts, designers, developers, testers, maintainers, and project managers), software vendors, and subcontractors.

The "other stakeholders" category can include parties both internal (e.g., people from legal, manufacturing, finance, sales, and support departments) and external (e.g., people from regulatory agencies, auditors, and the general public) to the project organization.

Continued on next page

Tip

A single stakeholder can belong to multiple categories. For example, a software product trainer can be a direct user (who needs to use the system as part of his or her job responsibility), an indirect user (who accesses training materials associated with the system), and an advisor (who provides advice on usability issues with a prior version of the software).

How do I do it?

1. **Identify stakeholders as either customers, users, or other stakeholders.**

   • List the stakeholders as roles in each of the categories, rather than as specific people. Remember that the same role might appear in multiple categories.

Tip

Use the generic stakeholder roles listed below as a starting point to help you categorize your stakeholders. Translate these generic roles into project-specific roles (e.g., for the CVGC project, the role "financial expert" would be "CVGC tax advisor") and categorize them.

   • Auditor

   • Buyer

   • Clerical user

   • Communications specialist

   • Contracts specialist

   • Cultural analyst

   • Customer service analyst

   • Database administrator

- Documentation analyst
- Environmental specialist
- Financial expert
- Future or possible direct user
- Government overseer
- Guest user
- Disabled user
- Hazardous materials specialist
- Help desk specialist
- Human resource specialist
- Legal expert
- Management reviewer
- Manufacturing specialist
- Marketing specialist
- Media consultant
- Multilingual user
- Operations staff
- Packaging specialist
- Payroll or salary specialist
- Procurement specialist
- Product installer
- Regulatory expert
- Report reviewer

- Sales specialist

- Safety inspector

- Scheduler

- System administrator

- System architect

- System user

- Security specialist

- Support specialist

- Technical writer

- Trainer

- Usability specialist

- User trainer

- Consider both internal and external stakeholders for each stakeholder category.

 For software that enforces regulations, be sure to include internal advisors who are well versed in the regulations, or identify external advisors who can adequately express the requirements.

- Enlist the project sponsor in identifying stakeholders.

 Do not launch your requirements effort without identifying at least one sponsor and one product champion and engaging them in the project. Strive for a single executive sponsor who will have the ultimate authority over the project and who will resolve requirements scope issues.

Be aware that direct users of the "as-is" system may become advisors if their jobs as system users are eliminated. As advisors, they can often provide useful information about flaws, inadequacies, and common problems with the "as-is" system.

 A common role in the "direct user" category will be a system administrator—someone who will grant, revoke, and change people's access to the system.

Roles in the "advisor" category often include people involved in training, regulatory, or legal areas inside or outside of your organization and in human resource organizations.

 As you define your stakeholders, be sure to focus on the "to-be" system—the system as it is envisioned. Keep the product vision in mind as you identify and categorize stakeholders. This will reduce the risk of regenerating the existing "as-is" system, rather than thinking about how the "to-be" software might be different or better.

2. **Review the list of stakeholder categories with the project stakeholders to ensure the list is complete and accurate.**

3. **Revise the list as needed and share it with the entire team.**

CVGC Stakeholder Categories

| Customers | | Users | | Other Stakeholders | |
Sponsor	Product Champion	Direct Users	Indirect Users	Advisors	Providers
• CEO	• Office manager	• Office manager • CEO • Estimator • Scheduler • Contracted window cleaners • Inventory supply managers • Customer callback liaison • Bookkeeper • Contractor hirer	• Credit card authorizers • Marketing manager • Advertising staff • Window supply vendors • Home-based business entrepreneurs	• CVCG tax advisor • Tax accountant • Residential real estate agents • Commercial real estate agents	• Project manager • Analyst • Developers • Database administrator

Links to other models

- Direct and indirect users can become actors in an actor table or *actor map*.
- Direct and indirect users can appear as external entities on a context diagram.

3.3   Stakeholder Profiles

What is it?

A *stakeholder profile* is a description that characterizes each stakeholder and explains his or her relationship to the project.

Alternative names for this tool

- Customer Profile
- User Profile
- Stakeholder Analysis

Why use it?

To understand the interests, concerns, and product success criteria for each of the system's stakeholders, to uncover potential sources of requirements conflict among stakeholders, and to highlight requirements topics that may need additional time and attention. Stakeholder profiles can also reveal potential obstacles for successful product implementation and help you define how much involvement each stakeholder should have in requirements elicitation.

What does it do?

- Educates the team about stakeholder expectations
- Provides the team with a high level understanding of user needs
- Uncovers contradictory stakeholder interests early in the project
- Highlights potential obstacles to stakeholder acceptance of the software

? *Key questions that this tool will answer*

- What are the stakeholders' key responsibilities with regard to the system being developed or changes being implemented?

- What motivations, desires, and hopes do stakeholders have for the software product?

- What software features or capabilities must be present for each stakeholder to view the product as a success?

- What obstacles, constraints, or limiting factors does each stakeholder foresee for himself or others that may threaten successful implementation?

- What level of comfort do stakeholders have with the technology?

- Are there any special working or environmental conditions that might impact the stakeholders' ability to effectively use the system?

How do I do it?

1. **Write a brief profile for each stakeholder. Describe his or her:**

   - **Role:** List the stakeholder category (e.g., sponsor, product champion, direct user, indirect user, advisor, or provider) that the stakeholder belongs to.

   - **Responsibilities:** Briefly describe each stakeholder's role as it relates to the project.

   - **Interests:** List the stakeholder's needs, wants, and expectations for the product (e.g., a sponsor's interests may include increased revenue, cost avoidance, improved services, and compliance with regulatory standards).

Software Requirements

- Success criteria: Describe the features or capabilities that the product must have to be viewed as successful.

- Concerns: List any obstacles, constraints, or limiting factors that might impede the project or inhibit stakeholder acceptance of the product.

- Technical proficiency: Describe the direct user's degree of familiarity with the technology.

- Work environment characteristics and constraints: Describe relevant working conditions that might affect system usage (e.g., a noisy work environment or mobile or outdoor usage).

2. **Include the stakeholder profiles in the user requirements document (if used) and the software requirements specification document.**

   - If the profiles contain a lot of information, document a profile for each stakeholder as a separate table or section in the appropriate requirements document.

Variations

3.3.1 Combining Categories

For small or less-complex projects, create a shorter version of the stakeholder profiles by combining the interests and success criteria categories.

CVGC Stakeholder Profiles

Stake-holder	Roles	Responsi-bilities	Interests	Success Criteria	Concerns	Technical Proficiency/Work Environment Constraints
CEO	• Sponsor • Indirect user	• Pay for the software project	• Increasing CVGC's job completion capacity • Attracting new contractors • Streamlining business operations	• Satisfies office manager's concerns • Reports on how the company is doing	• Adhering to state and federal tax laws • Having access to the new system as soon as possible	• N/A
Book-keeper	• Direct user • Advisor	• Close-out jobs • Manage accounts payable and receivable • Pay contractors	• Paying contractors quickly and accurately • Balancing books	• Generates accurate invoices • Balances books faster with less or no manual work • Minimizes contractor payment error complaints	• Transferring data from old to new system may be difficult • Learning the new system quickly • Handling successful IRS audits	• Bookkeeper is accustomed to manually writing checks and balancing books; less familiar with computer usage • Contractors often are waiting just feet away from the bookkeeper for a check

Continued on next page

Software Requirements

CVGC Stakeholder Profiles

Stake- holder	Roles	Responsi- bilities	Interests	Success Criteria	Concerns	Technical Proficiency/Work Environment Constraints
Sched- uler	• Direct user • Advisor	• Create, modify, and schedule jobs • Generate estimates • Dispatch contractors to jobs	• Generating esti- mates quickly with clients on the phone • Scheduling jobs within 5 days of request • Matching con- tractors to sites in their geographic region	• Eliminates double-booked jobs • Provides quick and accurate estimates	• Having easy-to-use scheduling screens • Handling the scheduling workload without additional staff • Fearing the scheduler's job will be eliminated if online estimating and schedul- ing is even- tually added into the software	• Scheduler is comfortable with current multiple screens process; does not trust computer to match contrac- tors with site locations • Scheduler often has people on telephone hold while doing estimates and schedules; high pressure (8 a.m.– 10 a.m. EST)

⬭⬭⬭ *Links to other models*

- Stakeholder responsibilities can describe actors in the actor table.
- The capabilities provided by the product (as listed in the "interests" and "success criteria" columns) suggest potential use cases.

Identified Combinations of Elicitation Techniques

You can combine a variety of elicitation techniques to ensure that you elicit the appropriate requirements from *all* of the relevant stakeholders. Some of the more-common techniques explored in this chapter include:

- Interviews with stakeholders
- Facilitated workshops
- *Exploratory prototypes*
- Focus groups
- Observation
- User task analysis
- Existing documentation study
- Surveys

Develop your elicitation plan by selecting and combining the applicable techniques from this list. For example, follow facilitated workshops with an exploratory prototype to find requirements errors and confirm the requirements, or follow observation with user task analysis to decide what to study and to focus on one task.

3.4 Interviews with Stakeholders

What are they?

Interviews with stakeholders are face-to-face meetings in which an interviewer asks questions to obtain information from the respondent. Interviews can be unstructured (with no predefined questions) or structured (with questions prepared in advance).

Why do it?

To collect general information about stakeholder needs, to ask customers and users to state their needs, and to help uncover conflicting software requirements. (Interviews can be useful when there are political, collocation, or scheduling barriers to gathering stakeholders together at the same time and place.)

What does it do?

- Identifies a broad range of requirements topics such as software usage modes (i.e., user tasks or needed data), priorities, user environment, and business goals
- Explores what the state of the business should be after the project is successfully completed
- Identifies additional sources of requirements information

How do I do it?

1. **Identify the people you would like to interview.**

   - Choose a cross section of people. Include sponsors, customers, and users with subject matter expertise.
   - Match the interviewees with interviewers that they are likely to be open with. Be sure that interviewers will be comfortable interviewing senior managers and customers, and vice versa. (**Note**: Interviewees

must see the interviewer as neutral and unbiased. Be aware of political, cultural, or organizational issues that might arise that could affect the interview process.)

2. **Prepare the interview questions.**

   • Clarify the goal of each interview (e.g., to gather background information and high-level features of the software, or to gain a detailed understanding of user work flow or data needs).

   • Construct the interview questions. Sequence them from general to more detailed. Arrange easier, factual questions (e.g., "What has been your involvement in this project so far?") at the beginning and more difficult, interpretive questions (e.g., "What obstacles to accomplishing work might this system present?") later in the interview.

 Tailor your opening questions to capture the interviewee's attention. For a senior manager or customer, ask, "Why is this project (or software) important to you (or your customers)?" or "What must this product do for you to call it a success?" For users who will interact directly with the software, say, "Tell me about your ideal way of <performing a task>?"

 Include *context-free questions* (i.e., high-level questions about both the product and the process) early in interviews and in all open-ended interviews. These types of questions allow you to understand the big picture. Examples include:

   • What problem does this system solve?

   • What problems could this system create?

   • What environment is this system likely to encounter?

   • What degree of precision is required or desired in this product?

Also include *metaquestions* (i.e., questions about questions) that allow you to adjust your questions during an interview. Examples include:

- Am I asking you too many questions?
- Do my questions seem relevant?
- Are you the right person to answer these questions?
- Who else might be able to answer these questions?
- Is there anything else I should be asking you?
- Is there anything you'd like to ask me?

[Reference 3: Gause and Weinberg, 1989]

3. **Schedule the interview and arrange the logistics for your meeting.**

- Find a location where the interview will not be interrupted.
- Prepare the interviewees. Provide them with the goals for the interview, and if possible, provide them with the interview questions a day or more in advance. Ask them to gather any documents (such as manuals, references, plans, or reports) that might be useful to refer to during the interview.
- Make sure that the interviewers are familiar with the terminology of the business. Share a glossary with the interviewees where appropriate, to ensure that they agree with the terms and definitions.
- Be sure to alert the interviewee as to how much time you expect the interview to take. (A typical interview will last forty-five to sixty minutes.)

 You can conduct an interview by telephone but you may miss the visual cues you would see in a face-to-face meeting. Use telephone interviews only as a last resort.

Interviews with Stakeholders 67

4. **Conduct the interview.**

  - Introduce yourself and ask an opening question.

  - Tell the interviewee that you will be taking notes during the interview. If you are doing a telephone interview, tell the interviewee that he or she may hear you typing notes.

  - Practice active listening. For example, repeat back answers in your own words and keep your eyes engaged with the interviewee.

  - Avoid leading questions (such as "Don't you think that..." or "Why don't you just...").

  - Be flexible, asking new or follow-up questions as needed.

  - Close each interview with a thank you, and describe the steps you will take next. Ask permission to ask follow-up questions if needed.

5. **Document the results.**

  - Review your notes immediately after the interview, while the information is still "fresh" in your mind.

  - Follow up with the interviewee to resolve any conflicting information.

  - Analyze your notes from multiple interviews to uncover patterns and conflicts.

  - Generate a set of models or textual requirements for initial review by the team, based on the interviews.

Audio taping and videotaping may seem efficient, but are usually not. The time it takes to listen to or watch each interview and take notes is not well spent. Use taping only if you want to learn about interviewing styles or if verbatim comments are important to your project. If you decide to record interviews, get permission from the interviewee beforehand.

Interviews involve obtaining information serially (i.e., one user or customer at a time). This results in a longer elapsed time than group-based techniques. This delay is compounded when you have to resolve conflicts by going back to interviewees multiple times. Moreover, results can be inconsistent with different interviewers or when interviewers filter the information provided. To save time and increase overall collaboration among stakeholders, consider gathering key stakeholders in a facilitated workshop (described below).

3.5 Facilitated Workshops

What is it?

A facilitated workshop is a gathering of carefully selected stakeholders who work together under the guidance of a skilled, neutral facilitator to produce and document requirements models.

[Reference 4: Gottesdiener, 2002]

Alternative names for this technique

- Joint Application Design or Development (JAD)
- Joint Requirements Planning (JRP)
- Design Workshop
- Domain Workshop
- Modeling Workshop
- Requirements Workshop
- Stakeholder Workshop

Why do it?

To quickly and efficiently define, refine, prioritize, and reach closure on user requirements. A workshop commits users to the requirements discovery process and promotes user ownership of the deliverables and, ultimately, of the system.

What does it do?

- Surfaces conflicting requirements in a safe environment
- Promotes trust and sharing of information
- Enables team members to obtain an overall view of the product requirements in large or complex projects
- Enables team members to partition the project into smaller projects to enable *incremental delivery* of the software (i.e., multiple releases of the software product produced over time)

How do I do it?

1. **Determine the workshop's purpose and participants.**

   - Write a concise workshop purpose statement (e.g., "to define the scope" or "to detail user requirements").
   - Draft a subset of requirements statements or analysis models before the workshop (if possible) to use as a starting point.
   - Define the roles (e.g., participants (users and subject matter experts), facilitator, recorder, sponsor, and observers) that people will take in the workshop. Clarify with each participant his or her role in the workshop and your expectations for his or her participation in the workshop process. (Allow testers, new analysts, and new business team members to learn about the requirements and the business domain by acting as recorders.)

Having the right people in the workshop is crucial. Make sure that participants have the right subject matter expertise to deliver the requirements and meet your purpose. The people who are most critical to the day-to-day business operations are often exactly the people you need in the workshop.

If the purpose of the workshop is to define the scope of the requirements or reach closure on high-level requirements, make sure that the sponsors take part. However, because sponsors often do not possess detailed knowledge of requirements, do not ask them to participate in detailed requirements workshops.

• Keep the workshop small. Strive for a dozen or fewer participants.

• Use a skilled, neutral facilitator, especially if you have a large group or there are many political issues or conflicts involved. A highly experienced facilitator will anticipate obstacles and plan accordingly.

• Have the facilitator interview some or all of the participants before the workshop, to learn enough to plan the workshop and confirm its purpose.

Facilitated requirements workshops can last anywhere from two hours to several days. Consider conducting multiple workshops if the purpose is broad, the time is short, or the group is large. If possible, plan to conduct several partial-day workshops to reduce the risk of draining participants' energy in long, multiple-day workshops. Between workshop sessions, have participants create interim deliverables (such as preliminary analysis models) or prioritize requirements lists in preparation for the next workshop.

2. **Identify the workshop's ground rules.**

- Have the facilitator gather ideas for ground rules from participants at the start of the workshop (or before the session begins, if possible). Example ground rules include:

  - Start and end on time.
  - Be prepared.
  - Focus on interests and not positions.
  - Share all relevant information.
  - Participate!

- Confirm the ground rules. Make sure that the participants own and enforce the ground rules, with help from the facilitator. During the workshop, have the facilitator help the group periodically check on adherence to the ground rules and revise the rules as needed.

- Define decision rules and a decision-making process for the workshop (which can be included with the ground rules). A decision rule is the rule the participants will follow when making a decision. Example decision rules include "The person-in-charge makes the final decision after consulting the group" and "The team will reach a final decision through consensus." Clarify the decision rules with the participants before making decisions.

Have the facilitator provide a process for leading the group through decision making in the workshop and obtain agreement on the decision-making process from the participants and workshop sponsors before the workshop starts (or, at the latest, at the start of the workshop).

---

3. **Define the workshop deliverables.**

   - Include tangible deliverables (such as analysis models) as well as intangible items (such as decisions).

   - Determine how you will know when the deliverables are good enough. Make these deliverables as specific as possible. Specific examples include:

     - The ability to "step through" analysis models developed in the workshop with user acceptance tests.

     - Obtaining mostly "yes" answers on a requirements specification inspection checklist when inspecting requirements. (See Appendix D for more information on the requirements specification inspection checklist.)

     - Obtaining participants' agreement that the requirements that matter to them have been described in sufficient detail to proceed to the next step in requirements development.

4. **Design the agenda.**

   - Create an agenda that opens the workshop, conducts requirements discovery activities, and then closes the workshop. Design specific activities after the opening so that participants progressively generate multiple requirements representations.

   - Send the agenda to participants before the session.

   - Ask participants to bring relevant business documents (e.g., reports, procedures, user documentation, and forms) with them to the workshop.

Do not overpromise what early workshops can deliver. Recognize that groups need to *form* (i.e., gain an understanding of their mutual purpose and goals) before they can *perform* (i.e., become productive).

5. **Conduct the session.**

   - Ask the project sponsor or a senior stakeholder to open the session by briefly describing the purpose of the workshop, conveying an appropriate sense of urgency and importance about the participants work together, and describing his or her commitment to the group's work.

   - Plan to use various interaction modes with the participants. Have them interact with the whole group and in small groups. Also have participants work alone at times to list, prioritize, or review group deliverables. Have people work in different small groups to learn from those who have different expertise. As participants become more productive, use multiple concurrent subgroups to elicit requirements models.

   - Use a variety of media and tools (including index cards, sticky notes, markers, and posters) to keep people interested throughout the session.

   - Use *scenarios* (to convey examples or *stories* of system usage) to step through other requirements models (such as the use cases, business rules, and data model described in Chapter 4) and help uncover missing or erroneous requirements during workshops.

   - Use a laptop computer, data projector, and printer so participants can review information immediately and the team can use the information for workshop-following assignments. Combine real-time recording with inexpensive, easy-to-use tools (such as sticky notes and index cards on the room's walls) to accelerate the elicitation process inside the workshop. Tape long sheets of poster paper onto walls or pin a large cloth that you have sprayed with repositionable adhesive, to allow participants to easily move cards around the wall. Photograph the room and walls with a digital camera and make the pictures available to the entire team.

Software Requirements

- Conduct short workshop retrospectives periodically throughout the workshop to get feedback on the workshop.

- Print workshop deliverables as you create them and check the deliverables for completeness and understanding before adding more details to them.

- Ask the sponsor and key stakeholders to join you for a "show-and-tell session" at the end of the workshop (or series of workshops) to allow participants to briefly present their deliverables and share issues that need resolution. (In addition to informing sponsors about key requirements issues, the show-and-tell session permits participants to reflect on their work and take satisfaction in their accomplishments.)

- Close the workshop by assigning any outstanding issues to specific participants with due dates and communication plans. Define the next steps to be taken and conduct a final workshop retrospective.

Ask users and customers to write a "vision" story for the idealized, perfect future. This story might begin with the user arriving at work and then having a productive day, including his or her interactions with software. (Participants can create these stories individually or in small groups.) Read the stories aloud and ask participants to identify the requirements missing from those generated in the workshop but present in one or more story.

Include an activity to discover the "Voice of the Customer." *[Reference 5: Pardee, 1996]* The Voice of the Customer includes the needs and wants of the software's customers and users. Use the Voice of the Customer to uncover requirements and understand the importance of these requirements to the stakeholders. If you have already generated requirements, use the Voice of the Customer to uncover any missing requirements.

Begin with stakeholder categories. (If these are not available, ask participants to generate a list of them as part of the workshop). Then, for each stakeholder category, list short requirements statements for:

- The things that users tell you they want in the product ("Spokens").

- The things that users will take for granted and will be dissatisfied about if they are not present in the product ("Expectors"). (Be aware that users may not think of expectors, may not know what they are, or may not want to reveal them.)

- The things that users will find attractive or exciting ("Delighters"). (Delighters may be latent or hidden wants that will make the product unique but if not present, will not be noticed.)

 Have users "role-play" to model requirements representations (i.e., have users act out a particular scenario or task). Document the steps the users perform, and play out multiple scenarios to derive use cases, data models, and business rules. (See Chapter 4 for more information on these requirements representations.)

6. **Follow up on issues, next steps, and actions.**

- Make the participants responsible for following up on any assigned tasks.

- Evaluate the workshop after completing the requirements elicitation. Analyze its usefulness to the requirements elicitation process and its value to the overall project. Use this information to adapt your requirements workshop practices.

Software Requirements

In addition to conducting workshops for projects that develop or buy software for internal use, commercial software development efforts can conduct facilitated workshops by having surrogate users participate or by running workshops at customer sites.

 If the project's scope is unclear, conduct a scope definition workshop before diving into detailed requirements. Have participants generate their ideal wish list of requirements, using requirements scope representations such as a context diagram or a preliminary list of use cases. Then, using an agreed-upon prioritization scheme, filter the large set of wished-for requirements into a realistic scope.

Variations

3.5.1 Prototype Reviews

Integrate peer reviews of *prototypes* into your requirements workshops. (See section 6.1 for more information on peer reviews.)

3.6 Exploratory Prototypes

What are they?

Exploratory prototypes are partial or preliminary versions of the software created to explore or validate requirements.

 Alternative names for this technique
- Mock-Up
- Storyboard

Why do it?

To allow users to give feedback early in the project and actively co-develop requirements with analysts.

What does it do?

- Provides a partial and preliminary version of the software as a mock-up using paper, whiteboards, or software tools
- Inexpensively demonstrates a subset of the product's functionality, user navigation, or interfaces between systems
- Makes abstract concepts more concrete and requirements more tangible
- Provides a shared work product upon which technical and businesspeople can collaborate

 Tip In addition to being useful for exploring requirements, prototyping is one of the best ways to validate requirements. Presenting prototype interfaces step-by-step, using scenarios (see section 4.7.4) or user acceptance tests (see section 6.2), confirms necessary task flows and uncovers missing requirements.

What types of prototypes are there?

Horizontal and vertical prototypes address the content of the proposed system differently. *Horizontal prototypes* mimic the user interfaces or a shallow portion of the system's functionality. *Vertical prototypes* dive into the details of the interface, the functionality, or both.

After you create a prototype, you can discard it (a throwaway prototype) or you can use it as the basis

Continued on next page

for developing the final system (an evolutionary prototype). Throwaway prototypes tend to be less expensive and faster to create than evolutionary prototypes. A throwaway prototype's purpose is to generate information, so it is developed using inexpensive, easy-to-use tools. Evolutionary prototypes tend to be more costly and time-consuming to create because they are built on a solid architectural foundation that will be retained for design and implementation.

Types of Prototypes

	Throwaway	Evolutionary
Horizontal	• Clarify functional requirements • Identify missing functionality • Explore user interface or navigation approaches	• Implement important use cases • Implement additional use cases based on priority • Refine Web sites • Adapt the system to rapidly changing needs
Vertical	• Demonstrate technical feasibility of performance, usability, or other quality attributes	• Implement complex software communication (e.g., Web-based or client-server) functionality and layers • Implement and optimize core algorithms • Test and tune performance

[Reference 8: Wiegers, 2003]

An exploratory prototype is usually a horizontal mock-up developed to crystallize unclear requirements, understand rapidly changing requirements, and explore user interface navigation approaches. Most exploratory prototypes are throwaways.

How do I do it?

1. **Select a portion of the product's scope to prototype.**
   - Choose requirements that are unclear, conflicting, or involve complex user interactions.
   - Choose a small set of functionality.
   - Use any available textual requirements or other requirements representations (such as use cases or events from analysis in Chapter 4).

2. **Determine whether you will create a throwaway prototype or evolutionary prototype.**
   - Clarify the purpose of the prototype with users and team members.
   - Establish the technical environment for developing the prototype, if appropriate.

3. **Design and build the prototype.**
   - Use real customer data (not fictitious data), if possible. (Be careful about privacy or security issues when using real data.) When building user interfaces, consider adding example data that will be realistic to users who are testing the prototype.

4. **Conduct the prototype evaluations with users.**
   - Begin with a statement about the goals of the prototype and next steps.
   - Demonstrate or simulate a user interacting with the system. Show mock-ups of the top-level interfaces in sequence.
   - Record user issues and suggestions.
   - Conduct the prototype review in two hours or less.
   - Create a summary of the findings and next steps, and agree upon a schedule for the next review (if necessary).

Tip Supplement prototype reviews with *walk-throughs* (i.e., have developers present, discuss, and step through a prototype using user-generated test cases (such as scenarios or user acceptance tests) to obtain feedback on the flow and to find missing or difficult steps or errors in the prototype).

Tip Use prototype reviews to clarify and elaborate user requirements models such as the data model, use cases, and business rules. Be sure that analysts have the draft models at hand and that they make notes during the reviews about necessary corrections and omissions that emerge during the prototype review. Include photographs or screen shots of the prototypes in requirements documents.

5. **Document the results.**

   • Correct any related models and requirements documents.

Beware! Because exploratory prototypes are often developed using different tools than those used to generate the deployed software, be careful not to allow users or team members to draw conclusions about the expected performance of the final product based on the performance of the prototype.

3.7 Focus Groups

What are they?

Focus groups are carefully planned group interviews that raise issues and ask open-ended questions to obtain information from participants. They often consist of a series of meetings between a moderator and groups of six to twelve people, usually with common demographics. Participation is voluntary and findings are kept confidential. In some cases, focus group participants are paid a small fee.

Why do it?

To obtain user reaction to new products or product ideas in a controlled environment, and to reveal subjective information and perceptions about product features. Focus groups explore requirements choices and obtain reactions to new components and interfaces. They also help product development organizations prioritize requirements and identify areas for further qualitative or quantitative study.

How do I do it?

1. **Define the objectives and target participants of the focus group.**

   - Decide whether you are looking for a general reaction to new or existing features or if you want to focus on specific capabilities.

   - Determine the target participants and geographic location for the session.

   - Decide how many sessions you will hold and their duration. Each session typically lasts from 90 to 150 minutes, but you should allow time for follow-up questions and unstructured discussion, if necessary.

   - Develop the questions to be asked.

2. **Plan and arrange the logistics for the session.**

   - Hold the session close to the participants' work or home, or at a natural gathering area such as a user conference.

   - Be sure the room is large enough for all participants to sit comfortably.

   - Define the ground rules for the session. Keep the ground rules short and to the point.

   - Arrange the chairs so that participants can see each other to encourage interaction.

   - Provide refreshments, if possible.

3. **Conduct the focus group.**

 • Introduce the participants and moderator, and review the ground rules.

 • Obtain consent before you videotape or audio tape the focus group, and explain how the session will be recorded.

 • Summarize the answers as participants address each question.

 • Stick to the allotted time.

 Have the moderator or a separate recorder capture answers and comments on flipcharts or electronically, and post the comments in full view of the participants, allowing them to correct misinterpretations.

4. **Analyze and document the collected information.**

 • Summarize the results of all of the focus group questions.

 • Share the results with the participants if this was promised or if they request it.

 • Use the information to confirm directions, explore new capabilities or features, determine where to focus further requirements gathering, or prioritize requirements.

Variations

3.7.1 Exploratory Focus Groups

Conduct an exploratory focus group by asking open-ended questions about an existing product and then asking participants to imagine a better product in the future. Ask them to describe its use, functionality, and characteristics.

3.8 Observation

What are they?

Observations are visits by requirements analysts to users' workplaces to watch users perform their jobs. Analysts can ask questions to clarify what tasks the users are performing or why they are performing the tasks; users explain their tasks as they perform their work. *[Reference 2: Beyer and Holtzblatt, 1998]*

Alternative names for this technique

- Contextual Inquiry
- Field Observation
- Ethnography
- Shadowing
- Soft Systems Analysis
- Social Analysis

Why do it?

To allow analysts and developers to understand how users will use the software in its work context. Observation can surface environmental issues in the users' workplace that will affect requirements. It also uncovers details that might not be obvious when users explain their tasks, because users' work is often intuitive to them and therefore difficult to articulate to others.

What does it do?

- Explores a broad range of requirements topics, including software usage (i.e., user tasks, needed data, and work flow), priorities, user environment, and business goals
- Builds trust between analysts and users

How do I do it?

1. **Identify the users that you want to observe.**

    • Decide how many users to observe.

    • Select users to observe. (Include both novice and expert users.) Include users who handle complex tasks that require automation. Select users who are willing to be observed and with whom the team wants to form good working relationships.

 Having technical people observe users in their work environment is an excellent way to build trusting relationships.

2. **Arrange for the observation.**

    • Arrange to observe a complete set of tasks or an end-to-end business process (which may require several observation sessions).

    • Contact users prior to the day of observation to allow them to become familiar with the person who will observe them, and answer any questions they may have (which will help reduce any stress or anxiety about the process). Request permission to ask occasional unobtrusive questions.

3. **Conduct the observation.**

    • Limit each observation to three hours or less (to avoid disrupting users' "real work").

    • Ask the user interacting with the software to describe what he or she is doing and why.

    • Take notes during the observation.

    • Ask the user if you can return or call to resolve any follow-up questions that you may have.

4. **Analyze and document your observations.**

    • Create and refine user requirements models shortly after each observation, while the information is still fresh in your mind.

Videotaping can be useful to allow multiple analysts or technical people to see users doing their work, but it can be costly and time-consuming and requires user permission. Use it sparingly.

Variations

3.8.1 Analyst Apprentice

An analyst may act as an apprentice, performing a user's tasks under the supervision of an experienced and knowledgeable user. The "analyst apprentice" will learn users' needs by doing the actual work and surface needs that might be "second nature" to an experienced user.

3.9   User Task Analysis

What is it?

User task analysis uses real or made-up examples to describe user tasks and the context within which the work will be performed. Users describe simulated uses of the system by recalling or imagining stories, episodes, or scenarios that they have experienced. Each user task is a stereotypical description, written in text form, of the use of the system to complete a task.

 Alternative names for this technique
- Role Modeling
- Scenario-Based Engineering
- Scripting
- Stimulus-Response Sequences
- Task Scripts
- Usage Analysis

Why do it?

To use examples rather than abstractions to elicit requirements, and to reveal requirements that users may have difficulty recalling outside of their work environment. User task analysis documentation can provide a basis for developing use cases, conducting *model validation*, developing user acceptance tests, and designing prototypes.

What does it do?

- Allows users to explain their needs with realistic examples
- Groups similar tasks into logical sets of functional requirements
- Describes normal system uses as well as those in which errors may occur or unusual steps need to be taken
- Specifies event sequences as narratives or numbered lists

How do I do it?

1. **Identify and document the user roles.**

   - Survey the user community to understand the types of people who do the work, their background, and their typical work habits and preferences.
   - Arrange to meet with users in their work environment.
   - Decide whether you want to do task analysis of the "as-is" system, the "to-be" system, or both.
   - Prepare users by explaining what you will be asking them to do. Ask them to think of examples to share during the meeting.

Tip If possible, precede task analysis with observation. (User task analysis inherently involves observation.) You can ask more-focused questions during task analysis if you are already familiar with the basic steps users must perform.

2. **At the meeting, ask users to describe typical tasks that they must accomplish with the system.**

   • Ask for two to five examples of the same or similar tasks, listening for differences in the steps, if any.

Tip Ask, "What is a typical day in the life of <user role>?" Alternatively, ask users to role-play performing a specific task (such as creating an estimate), and have them talk through each step (i.e., "First I find the site, and then I ask which location the customer wants cleaned. Next, I check the last time that location was cleaned...").

   • Always address the normal, most typical tasks first, in which no errors or variations occur. After documenting those tasks, explore the alternative steps needed to handle errors or variations.

   • Take notes. Do not try to capture every detail. Ask clarifying questions and repeat back the steps or sentences as users describe them.

Tip During discussions with users, ask questions to uncover the nonfunctional requirements related to each task (e.g., how often the task is done, where the users who perform the task are located, what reference materials are used in completing the task, how many users perform the task, and what the peak times are for performing the task).

3. **Document the user tasks.**

   • Write (or ask users to write) one task step per sticky note or index card and ask users to arrange them in sequence on a wall, or capture the task informa-

tion on a laptop and display what is being recorded
using a data projector.

- Document a few sentences as a numbered list of four
  to seven steps for each task. Supplement the task
  narrative or numbered steps with a visual diagram
  (such as a flowchart) to show the user's steps.

 Tip You can document user tasks in the format of
"goal/tasks/actions." The goal is the user's intent,
the tasks are the steps you will take to meet the
goal, and the actions are the discrete events that
comprise each task.

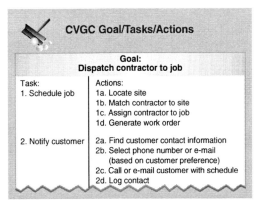

CVGC Goal/Tasks/Actions

Goal:
Dispatch contractor to job

Task:	Actions:
1. Schedule job	1a. Locate site
	1b. Match contractor to site
	1c. Assign contractor to job
	1d. Generate work order
2. Notify customer	2a. Find customer contact information
	2b. Select phone number or e-mail (based on customer preference)
	2c. Call or e-mail customer with schedule
	2d. Log contact

 Tip Do not expect to explore all tasks in a single
meeting, especially when eliciting requirements
for large, complex systems. Iteratively develop
the tasks over days or weeks if necessary. Ask
users to evaluate the task documentation before
subsequent meetings, and then start by reviewing
errors and omissions before launching into
additional tasks.

- Identify the details that might go into user requirements models (such as the data model and business rules).

- Test the task sequences with scenarios to uncover missing steps.

- Review the user profiles from the stakeholder profiles (described in section 3.3). Check that descriptions of direct users accurately portray typical users now that user tasks are more clearly defined.

- Follow up with users to clarify any unanswered questions.

4. **Develop related user requirements models and specify the quality attributes.**

   - Draft the user requirements models. (See Chapter 4 for more information on user requirement models.)

Variations

3.9.1 Scenarios and Evolutionary Prototypes

Have developers create an evolutionary prototype for each scenario.

3.9.2 User Task Analysis and User Acceptance Tests

Write user acceptance tests for each task. (See section 6.2 for more information on user acceptance tests.) Have developers create prototypes and test each user task with test cases as they develop the code.

3.9.3 Ask Why Five Times

As users explain the task, ask "why?" up to five times in succession to verify the necessity of each task. (This can reveal erroneous user assumptions or detect unnecessary or obsolete business rules.)

Software Requirements

3.10 Existing Documentation Study

What is it?

An existing documentation study is an inspection of existing document sources to uncover requirements information.

 Alternative names for this technique
- Market Analysis
- Requirements Reuse

Why do it?

To discover or verify requirements using a low-cost technique. A documentation study enables the team to define features provided in a competitor's software (in commercial software projects) and to surface requirements to allocate to people rather than to software (in all types of projects). Studying documentation can also provide requirements information when you are replacing an existing system.

What does it do?

- Reuses existing software-related documentation to provide a starting point for functionality that could be included in the product
- Permits reverse-engineering of requirements and other software deliverables from existing documents
- Reveals functionality and quality attributes needed by a commercial software product to be competitive
- Uncovers business rules that the software might need to enforce

---

How do I do it?

1. **Identify the appropriate documentation sources to use.**

   - Ask systems and support staff what documentation exists and whether it is accurate. Use only reliable documentation to uncover requirements and generate analysis models.

   - Locate user documentation that could be in physical form (e.g., training manuals and procedural guidelines) as well as in soft form (e.g., help screens and error messages).

 Consider using:

   - Backup documentation (e.g., business continuity documents).

   - Recovery documentation (e.g., disaster recovery documents).

   - Help screens.

   - Job descriptions.

   - Operation manuals and guidelines.

   - Strategic and business plans.

   - Regulations, industry standards, and company policies.

   - Published reviews of COTS software in technical journals.

   - Standard operating procedures (SOPs).

   - Systems documentation (including prior user requirements documents, user specification documents, and specifications of interfacing systems and subsystems).

- Support documentation (e.g., help desk, field support, and installation, maintenance, and troubleshooting guides).

- User problem reports, complaint logs, and enhancement requests.

- Training materials, user manuals, and tutorials.

- Web sites and marketing literature of competing products.

- Online user and discussion groups.

• Search for information on competing products, especially those with functionality that is appealing to customers, most utilized, least utilized, troublesome, or missing.

2. **Review and analyze the documentation.**

• Look for patterns that suggest valuable functionality for the new system.

• Search for information about nonfunctional requirements (e.g., performance, usability, and security).

• Consider which potential requirements you will allocate to software and which you will allocate to people as part of a business process.

• Share and review the findings with customers and users.

• Use the information to identify areas for further exploration and to uncover missing requirements from a set of already drafted requirements.

Examining diverse sources of documentation can be time-consuming. Prioritize and select the most useful resources. Materials that provide a sound starting point or that can fill in gaps in requirements are good candidates for study.

3. **Create draft analysis models.**

   - Use the information from this study to draft analysis models such as a context diagram, a list of use cases, and a data model. (See Chapter 4 for more information on analysis models.)

   - Use the information to begin to draft specifications. (See Chapter 7 for more information on drafting specifications.)

3.11 Surveys

What is it?

A survey is a method of gathering information anonymously from a large number of users. A survey can be open-format (permitting respondents to add information on their own and possibly provide unexpected and insightful feedback) or closed-format (with fixed responses, making them faster to answer and easier to analyze).

Alternative names for this technique

- Market Surveys

- Questionnaires

Why do it?

To inexpensively sample users for their reaction to an existing product or proposed requirements. Surveys allow you to quickly analyze user responses and unobtrusively obtain requirements from users who are generally inaccessible. Surveys can help you obtain subjective information (such as a customer's satisfaction with a product or its performance) and information about the relative importance of various features.

What does it do?

- Reveals sources of user satisfaction and dissatisfaction with a current product
- Provides data for statistical analysis from a large number of users
- Supplies subjective and demographic information from users

How do I do it?

1. **Identify the purpose of the survey.**

   - Determine a discrete goal (e.g., obtaining feedback on proposed features).

    When replacing existing software, be sure that you understand the functionality and quality attributes currently being satisfied, to help you focus your survey goal.

2. **Determine the sample group and the method of collection.**

   - For small groups (i.e., 150 or fewer), consider surveying everyone. For a very large group (i.e., thousands), sample a subset of the user community.

Tip

You may want to segment the customers into different user categories and use questions focused on each segment. (Be sure to use a statistically valid sample size for each segment.) Some sample segments include:

- User base size (e.g., "large corporate users" or "small companies").

- Frequency of usage (e.g., "occasional users: twice a week" or "power users: daily usage for two or more hours").

- Components used (e.g., "reporting and querying users" or "system administrators").

- Decide if your survey will be a mailed (paper) survey, an online (Web-based) survey, an e-mail survey, a telephone survey, or an on-site survey (i.e., administered at the customer's location).

3. **Design the survey questions.**

- Decide if you will use subjective survey questions, objective survey questions, or both. Questions can be multiple choice, open-ended numeric (leaving it to users to input the number), or open-ended text (allowing users to enter free-form text).

- Construct unbiased questions. Consider adding slightly different versions of the same questions to verify the repeatability of the responses.

- Ask short, unambiguous questions. Avoid slang, questions with the word "not" in them, and leading questions that presume an answer.

- Be sure that each question addresses a single issue. (A question like "Rate the response time and usability of the query function" addresses two issues, not one.)

Software Requirements

- Start with easy questions that arouse the interest of respondents.

- Group similar questions.

- Use transitional statements when moving to a new topic.

- Limit the number of questions. (Shorter surveys get higher response rates.)

 Skillful survey design is essential. Be sure that you sharply define the survey goals, create unbiased questions, and consider the means for statistically analyzing the data as part of your overall design. Some additional considerations include:

- Make the survey attractive-looking.

- For open-ended text questions, leave adequate space for the answers.

- To measure subjective reactions, use ranking scales from best to worst or most preferred to least preferred (e.g., +2 = "Really want this," +1 = "Would like this," 0 = "Don't care," -1 = "Don't want this," -2 = "Would not use the product if this is included").

4. **Test the survey before you distribute it.**

- Include a few real respondents in your test.

- Review the validity and understandability of the questions with a sampling of people.

- Record how long it takes testers to complete the survey.

- Use the feedback to modify the questions, instructions, or cover letter.

---

5. Administer the survey.

- Send a prenotification letter or cover letter that explains:

  - Why the survey is being done.

  - Who is sponsoring the survey.

  - How the results will be used.

  - An incentive for respondents (e.g., a copy of the results or a token gift).

  - The need for a prompt response.

  - Your policy on confidentiality of responses.

  - Contact information for questions.

  (This letter may increase your response rate.)

- Include instructions and a cover letter or paragraph with your survey that provides a name and contact information in case respondents have questions.

- Make it convenient for respondents to return the survey.

Most surveys tend to have a low response rate so you may want to supplement the surveys with other elicitation techniques to ensure that you have enough information to proceed with your requirements development process.

---

6. **Analyze and document the data.**

   - Quantify the responses and have survey design experts mathematically test the reliability and repeatability of the results.

   - Use the information to confirm requirements choices or to learn where to focus further requirements development efforts.

   - Present the information to the requirements team in a viewer-friendly manner, such as in a bar chart, pie chart, or matrix.

 If you promised to show respondents the results, make sure that you do so!

 Conduct surveys only when you have the time and resources to carefully plan and design the sample questions and determine how you will evaluate the results. The cost of making decisions based on bad data is expensive.

Factors to consider

Each project is different. When selecting which requirements elicitation techniques to use, consider the factors from the tables on the following pages, to help ensure that your requirements elicitation is successful.

Continued on following page

Technique	Factors to Consider		
	Number of End Users	Accessibility to Subject Matter Experts	Time for Gathering Requirements
Interviews	Not feasible with large numbers of users and experts; use representatives.	Requires access to interviewees; can use telephone interviews, and clarify conflicting data can take days or weeks.	Total time to conduct interviews, collate findings, and clarify findings, although this limits the quality of the information gathered. Interviewers can travel to users who are not at the same location.
Exploratory prototypes	Select one or more representative user(s) from each user group.	Requires direct access to users for prototype reviews unless online tools are used for reviews. Ideally, prototyping is combined with facilitated workshops or user task analysis, which require direct access to users.	Exploratory prototypes that are discarded can be developed in hours, while evolutionary prototypes can take days or weeks. Reviews take only hours, once scheduled. Multiple reviews should be conducted as the prototype is iteratively developed.
Facilitated workshops	Select one or more representative user(s) from each user group.	Relies on face-to-face interaction to be most effective; usually requires multiple workshops within a short time frame. Users may have to travel to workshops.	Getting the right people for wellplanned workshops reduces the time to develop requirements to days or weeks and increases the quality of the requirements.

Continued on following page

Factors to Consider

Technique	Number of End Users	Accessibility to Subject Matter Experts	Time for Gathering Requirements
Focus groups	Select one or more representative user(s) from each user group.	Relies on face-to-face interaction; usually requires multiple focus group meetings.	Usually takes weeks to plan, conduct, and analyze the data.
Observation	Select one or more representative user(s) from each user group.	Relies on real-time access to users in their work environment. Observers can travel to user sites.	Can be done over days or weeks, depending on user accessibility.
User task analysis	Select one or more user(s) from each direct user group or external customers.	Relies on face-to-face interaction to be most effective. Usually requires meetings within a short time frame.	User meetings followed by documenting the tasks generally take days.
Existing documentation study	Not applicable.	Not applicable.	Analysis and documentation can take days or weeks.
Surveys	Useful for sampling a large number of stakeholders.	Physical access not required.	Designing the survey, obtaining responses, and summarizing the data can take weeks or months.

Continued on following page

Tip It is important to respect stakeholders' time when using techniques that involve direct stakeholder interaction. Make sure that you start and end on time when interviewing, facilitating workshops, holding focus groups, conducting user task analysis, or observing users.

Skills and characteristics needed

Regardless of which elicitation techniques you use, you will need solid analysis skills and an ability to be neutral. Additional skills and characteristics for each elicitation technique include:

Technique	Facilitation Skills	Interpersonal Skills	Interviewing Skills	Observing/Listening Skills	Technical Writing Skills
Interviews		X	X	X	
Exploratory prototypes	X				
Facilitated workshops	X	X	X		
Focus groups	X	X	X	X	
User task analysis		X	X	X	
Observation		X		X	
Existing documentation study					X
Surveys			X*		X

* If surveys are done on the telephone or face-to-face

3.12 Stakeholder Elicitation Plan

What is it?

A stakeholder elicitation plan is a plan that considers the importance of the various stakeholders' needs and their contributions to the requirements development process.

Alternative names for this tool

- Stakeholder Involvement Plan
- Stakeholder Inclusion Strategy

Why do it?

To decide who should be involved in the various requirements activities and how they should contribute. Developing such a strategy helps you avoid overlooking stakeholders and missing requirements. It also helps gain commitment from the stakeholders' for their time and involvement.

Stakeholder involvement is essential for successful software projects. People are the primary sources for requirements information so it is important to obtain early stakeholder involvement to focus on the right requirements as soon as possible. Eliciting the wrong requirements will have severe project consequences.

What does it do?

- Enables the team to focus its requirements efforts on high-priority stakeholders
- Builds collaborative relationships among technical people and project stakeholders

- Encourages sponsors and champions to ensure that people with critical requirements knowledge will be available to the project team
- Promotes the effective use of people's time

Key questions that this tool will answer

- How important are each stakeholder's needs?
- How should we involve each stakeholder in the requirements development process?

How do I do it?

1. **Rank the importance of each stakeholder in the stakeholder categories. Use a ranking scheme such as MoSCoW:**
   - Must (M): Essential to success
   - Should (S): Very important to gather and understand this stakeholder's requirements
   - Could (C): Good to have this stakeholder's involvement, but less important
   - Won't (W): Not to be considered

   [Reference 7: Stapleton, 1997]

2. **Determine how you will involve each stakeholder ranked as an M, S, or C. Consider:**
   - Degree of involvement: Decide the extent to which each stakeholder will participate. He or she may fully participate, have some degree of limited involvement, or be indirectly involved if a surrogate is representing his or her needs.

Beware!

Because access to external users may be difficult or unfeasible, product development, field support, or marketing staff often act as surrogate users for commercial software projects. Surrogate users may not adequately understand or represent the needs of the real users for whom they are standing in. Business managers need to be aware of the risk of using surrogates who have insufficient experience and knowledge to adequately represent user needs.

Be sure that you employ techniques that reduce the risks associated with using surrogates (e.g., supplement surrogate involvement in interviews or surveys with information from actual direct users).

- Method of involvement: Determine how the stakeholder will be involved:

  - Actively: Participates in requirements workshops, surveys, interviews, focus groups, or prototypes

  - Passively: Gets reports from surrogates or reviews e-mail messages about the progress of requirements development

  - Indirectly: Supplies help desk or customer request logs or provides anonymous survey or marketing data

- Frequency of involvement: Decide if the stakeholder will be continuously or periodically involved.

3. **Record the elicitation plan in a table or other document.**

CVGC
Stakeholder Elicitation Plan

Stakeholder Role	Importance	Degree of Involvement	Method of Involvement	Frequency of Involvement
CEO	Must (M)	Limited	Passive: Receive status reports via e-mail or short telephone conversations	Periodically: Weekly
Bookkeeper	Must (M)	Full	Active: • Interview for wish list requirements • Include in four half-day facilitated workshops to create analysis models • E-mail draft requirements documents	Continuously: Daily during weeks 2–4
Residential real estate agents	Could (C)	Limited	Active: Random telephone interviews about service marketing ideas	Periodically: Calls during business hours early in week 2

Variations

3.12.1 Stakeholder Influence and Importance

Analyze the stakeholder's influence (i.e., the degree of power each stakeholder has over the project) and importance (i.e., the degree to which each stakeholder's success criteria are essential to the project's goals) before defining a stakeholder elicitation strategy. *[Reference 6: Smith, 2000]*

Plot stakeholders along these dimensions in a simple XY graph. When planning stakeholder elicitation, make decisions about each stakeholder's involvement according to their respective influence and importance.

A suggested treatment for involving stakeholders is provided below.

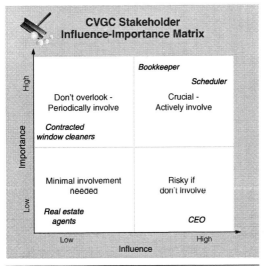

Use the elicitation plan to ensure that you involve a combination of stakeholders who:

- Are willing to collaborate in requirements elicitation.

- Are knowledgeable and experienced in the business domain (to ensure that you elicit valid requirements).

- Represent typical users, including novices (to uncover usability requirements).

- Have the authority to reach closure on requirements (to eliminate project delays).

- Are able to commit the time and energy to participate in requirements elicitation.

As you elicit requirements with your plan, ask stakeholders to review and correct the documented outcomes. Allow time to revise any necessary documentation based on the feedback that you receive. Share the documentation with team members and conduct peer reviews to ensure the documented requirements accurately describe user needs. Repeat the requirements elicitation cycle to deepen the team's understanding of requirements.

CHAPTER
4
Analyze the Requirements

To effectively analyze requirements, you need to sufficiently understand and define the requirements so stakeholders can prioritize their needs and allocate requirements to software.

Analysis results in requirements models. Requirements models (also referred to as analysis models) are user requirements represented by diagrams, structured text (such as lists, tables, or matrices), or a combination. Analysis also entails prioritizing requirements by analyzing trade-offs among the requirements to make decisions about their relative importance and timeliness.

Requirements elicited from stakeholders and articulated using analysis models need to be complete and clear enough to validate later in your software requirements process. (The requirements models you create here will supplement the requirements you specify as natural language declarative statements in the next chapter.)

Requirements analysis is primarily the responsibility of the analyst, but must involve key stakeholders such as users, customers, and technical staff who need to understand user needs.

Why should I create requirements models?

Requirements models will help you:

- Facilitate communication between technical and businesspeople. Models let the team look at different aspects of the user requirements from different perspectives.

- Uncover missing, erroneous, vague, and conflicting requirements. User requirements models link together, allowing your team to reveal related requirements and inconsistencies between models. Discovering and correcting these errors results in higher quality requirements.

- Make the requirements development process more interesting and engaging to stakeholders. Using both textual and visual models provides variety and permits stakeholders to understand requirements from more than one angle.

- Tap into different modes of human thinking. Some people think more precisely with words while others are better able to understand concepts with diagrams. Using both types of representations leverages different thinking modes.

The requirements analysis cycle

It is important to analyze the requirements as you elicit them from people, documents, and external sources. To analyze requirements:

1. **Model the business (if necessary).**
   - Determine if business modeling is needed.
   - Choose one or more business models.
   - Create the models, verifying their correctness as they evolve.

---

2. **Define the project scope.**
   - Create a combination of models to depict the project scope.
   - Check the models against each other to uncover requirements defects.
   - Review and obtain agreement from the project sponsor.

3. **Create detailed user requirements models.**
   - Select multiple models that will help users articulate their needs.
   - Iteratively refine the models, validating their correctness.
   - Leverage the stakeholder elicitation plan to make the best use of people's time.
   - Revise your scope models when newly understood requirements emerge.

4. **Prioritize the requirements.**
   - Organize requirements so they can be easily prioritized.
   - Gather stakeholders together to negotiate requirements trade-offs.
   - Determine criteria for making decisions about the relative importance of requirements.
   - Prioritize requirements based on those criteria.

5. **Repeat steps 3 and 4 as requirements details emerge or are revised.**

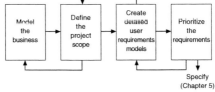

What models can I create?

You can use a variety of user requirements models to analyze requirements. The models represent answers to the "4W's + H" (*Who? What? When? Why? + How?*).

Focus Question	Example Questions	User Requirement Models for this Focus
Who	• Who are the project's stakeholders?	• Stakeholder categories
	• Who will directly interact with the system?	• Actor table (and possibly an actor map) or personas
	• Who will see what when they interact with the system?	• Dialog map (supplemented with or substituted by a prototype or dialog hierarchy)
What	• What do important business terms mean?	• Glossary
	• What functions in the organization interact to share information?	• Relationship map (a business model)
	• What information or assets go into and out of the system?	• Context diagram
	• What are the static data elements that must be stored and how are they related?	• Data model (supplemented with or substituted by a class model, data tables, or a data dictionary)
When	• When does the system need to respond or act?	• Event-response table
	• When do tasks get performed and when does information change?	• State diagram (supplemented with or substituted by a state-data matrix)
Why	• Why are we motivated to enforce standards, policies, regulations, and legislation?	• Business policies
	• Why are the decisions made that influence behavior and assert business structure?	• Business rules (supplemented with or substituted by decision tables or decision trees)

Continued on next page

Software Requirements

Focus Question	Example Questions	User Requirement Models for this Focus
How	• How do processes operate in the business to achieve business goals? • How are tasks performed and in what sequence?	• Process map (a business model) • Use cases and possibly use case maps and use case packages (supplemented with or substituted by scenarios, stories, activity diagrams of use cases, or data flow diagrams)

Note: A fifth "W"—*Where*—primarily provides information about nonfunctional requirements, specifically those related to the future operational and deployment environment. Because this chapter focuses on user requirements (which depict functional requirements), we will not discuss *Where* questions at this time.

The User Requirements Roadmap on the next page shows models you can use to analyze user requirements. The Roadmap includes models that are useful for analyzing the business (shown in italics) and others that clarify project scope. Stakeholder categories are defined early in the elicitation process to identify the people to involve in requirements modeling. High-level and detailed models are useful for revealing defects (e.g., errors, omissions, and conflicts).

 You can substitute alternative model representations when the alternatives better communicate requirements or better fit your project culture.

User Requirements Models Roadmap

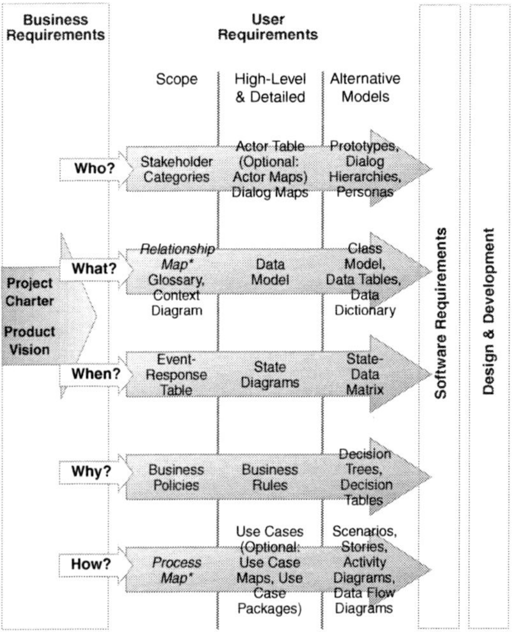

Business Requirements
User Requirements
Scope
High-Level & Detailed
Alternative Models
Who?
Stakeholder Categories
Actor Table (Optional: Actor Maps) Dialog Maps
Prototypes, Dialog Hierarchies, Personas
What?
Relationship Map* Glossary, Context Diagram
Data Model
Class Model, Data Tables, Data Dictionary
Project Charter
Product Vision
When?
Event-Response Table
State Diagrams
State-Data Matrix
Why?
Business Policies
Business Rules
Decision Trees, Decision Tables
How?
Process Map*
Use Cases (Optional: Use Case Maps, Use Case Packages)
Scenarios, Stories, Activity Diagrams, Data Flow Diagrams
Software Requirements
Design & Development

*Business Model

Adapted from Reference 4: Gottesdiener, 2002

How do I choose the right models?

Some requirements models are better suited to communicate requirements for certain business domains. Choose models that answer multiple focus questions (*Who, What, When, Why,* and *How*) to provide richer insight into requirements and develop the models accordingly. For example:

- Transactional business domains (which handle business processes and tasks such as business operations and administration, order processing, and inventory management) are well suited for *How* models (e.g., use cases and scenarios). Related *Who* and *Why* models (e.g., actors and business rules) are also useful for these domains.

- Structural domains (which exist to store and analyze data such as systems that mine data and generate queries and reports) are well suited for *What* models (e.g., data models). You should also supplement these models with *Why* models (e.g., business rules).

- Dynamic domains (which respond to continually changing events to store data and act on it based on its state at a point in time (e.g., systems that manage network trafficking, claim adjudication, mechanical device operations, and other real-time operations)) are well suited for *When* models (e.g., *event-response tables* and state diagrams) and *Why* models (e.g., business rules). You should include *What* models (e.g., a data model) and *Who* models when user interfaces are involved.

- Control-oriented domains (which test for conditions to take action or decisions such as logistics, fraud detection, product configuration, and diagnostics) are best described by *Why* models (e.g., business rules and *decision tables*) and should be supplemented by *What* models (e.g., data models).

Note: These are guidelines only. Each domain is different so you should determine which models are most useful by developing a subset of models in a preliminary form and validating them, then adjust your selections accordingly.

It is not necessary to use all of the user requirements models. You should choose a subset that is suitable for your project's problem domain. Save stakeholders time by drafting a few models at a high level, then checking with stakeholders to see if they are useful.

Be clear whether each model represents the "as-is" situation or the "to-be" requirements. When the current process, data, or system is not well understood, first create one or more "as-is" models. Avoid analysis paralysis by drafting the "as-is" situation at a scope or high level—just enough to understand the current environment while also ensuring that important requirements satisfied by the current system will also be included in the new system.

What Tools and Techniques Will I Use to Analyze Requirements?

When you need to:	Then create:
Model the business	Some combination of Relationship Map and/or Process Map
Understand the project scope	Some combination of Context Diagram, Event-Response Table, and/or Business Policies
Add detail to user requirements	Some combination or variation of Actor Table, Use Cases, Dialog Maps, Data Model, State Diagrams, and/or Business Rules
Negotiate trade-offs among requirements	Prioritized Requirements

Modeling the Business

Business modeling helps you understand how a software application will support business processes, and uncovers requirements that you need to allocate to businesspeople and business processes (e.g., updating official documents, reworking guidelines, conducting training, and revising standard operating procedures). A business process is a set of related tasks that creates something of value to the business. Business modeling also helps define efficient processes for using the new software.

The proposed software must integrate with existing or new manual business processes, but not all software projects require business modeling. You should consider business modeling when:

- The project scope is unclear or very large.

- There is unclear or diffused sponsorship.

- Business management wants to rethink or reengineer how work gets done.

- The project involves investigating or implementing COTS software.

- The business must conform to legal or regulatory policies that require manual intervention, processes, and documentation.

Business modeling requires sponsorship and customer involvement. Many software projects require significant business process and organizational change. When a business has regulatory or legal burdens, nonsoftware processes are necessary for survival, and jobs and roles often change. People need to be communicated with early and often. Businesspeople need to define and implement new procedures and documentation, as well as communicate and manage the change. Business modeling allows you to address these tough issues early on.

4.1   Relationship Map

What is it?

A relationship map is a diagram showing what information and products are exchanged among external customers, providers, and key functions in the organization.

 Alternative names for this model
- Business Interaction Model
- Organizational Context Diagram
- Organizational Relationship Map

Why use it?

To understand the organizational context for the project by identifying affected business functions and their inputs and outputs. A relationship map can reveal business process improvement opportunities before defining the scope of a software project.

What does it do?
- Illustrates what inputs and outputs the functions or parts of the organization send and receive to one another and to external entities
- Treats the overall business process as a set of interactions
- Helps businesspeople better understand cross-functional relationships and decide if business process change is warranted

 Key questions that this model will answer
- What inputs do we receive from our external customers and providers?
- What outputs do we provide to our external customers and providers?

- What functional areas are involved in handling those inputs and outputs?

- What are the handoffs (inputs and outputs) within our organization?

How do I do it?

1. **Draw the key functions, departments, and work groups involved in the business process as boxes.**

   - Choose business functions logically, not necessarily according to an organizational chart.

   - Err on the side of "more is better." For example, instead of describing a high-level function as "Sales," describe it by its subfunctions of "Market Research," "Lead Generation," and "Advertising." As you generate inputs and outputs, judge whether additional breakdown is needed.

   - Include "Customers" and "Providers," if applicable.

   - Consider functions that include Accounting, Sales, Marketing, Research & Development, Finance, Engineering, Manufacturing, Production, Inventory Management, Distribution, Customer Service, Regulatory, Human Resources, and Legal.

2. **List the key inputs and outputs that each function receives or produces.**

   - Consider reports, files, test results, policies and procedures, revenues, budgets, financial information, designs, referrals and leads, products, invoices, and any other tangible inputs and outputs.

   - Use high-level names (e.g., "cleaning materials" rather than "towels," "cleaning fluid," "squeegee," "ladder," and "bucket").

---

3. **Connect the inputs and outputs to the functions that use and produce them.**

- Use arrowheads to indicate the flow direction.
- Label each arrow with the name of the input or output.
- Qualify the names of files and reports with adjectives that further describe them (e.g., "Lead generation report" or "Monthly commission file").

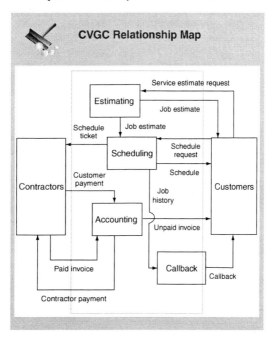

CVGC Relationship Map

* Inputs and outputs might become inputs and outputs on a context diagram.

* Customers and providers might be external entities on a context diagram.

* Functional areas might be lanes in a process map.

Variations

4.1.1 Business Process Improvement

Use the relationship map to identify business process improvement opportunities before starting a software effort. Look for:

 Overloaded functions: a large number of inputs and outputs throughout the diagram.

 Repetition: the same or similar input or output used in multiple functions.

 Multiple external interfaces: many inputs and outputs across functions going to and from external customers and providers.

 Naked functions: missing inputs or outputs.

4.2 Process Map

What is it?

A process map shows the sequence of steps, inputs, and outputs needed to handle a business process across multiple functions, organizations, or job roles.

Alternative names for this model

- Swimlane Diagram
- Cross-Functional Process Map
- Line of Visibility Model (LOVEM)

Why use it?

To identify which processes are allocated to the business (manual processes) and which will be allocated to software. Process maps also serve as a basis for business process improvement.

What does it do?

- Provides a cross-functional view of a single business process
- Illustrates automation points in a process
- Enables businesspeople to consider changes to documentation, existing work flow, work aids, decisions, and handoffs, to improve an existing business process
- Provides a framework for adding business process reengineering metrics

Key questions that this model will answer

- What is the flow of work needed to create something of value to the business?
- What functional areas, departments, or job roles are involved in the process?
- What triggers the overall process?

- What specific steps are needed and what is the sequence of the steps?

- Where decisions are made, and by whom?

- What are the handoffs (inputs and outputs) of each step?

How do I do it?

1. **Name the business process to be modeled, starting with an action verb.**

2. **Define the *business event* that triggers or starts the process.**

   - Name the business event in a "subject + verb + object" format (e.g., "Customer places order").

 Remember that business events can be unpredictable with respect to timing and frequency (e.g., receipt of a phone call, receipt of an invoice, approval of a loan, or receipt of a signal from a monitor).

3. **Name the end point or outcome of the process.**

   - Give it a simple and direct name, stated in the positive (e.g., "Order is complete," "Job is scheduled," or "Invoice is paid").

   Note: The process ends after the entire process produces something(s) of value to the business or its customers.

4. **List the participants in the business process (i.e., functional areas, departments, or roles) in a column along the left side of the diagram.**

5. **Create horizontal rows or "lanes" for each participant, to represent the organizational entity or role where the work is done.**

   - Place the lane most involved in the process as the top lane on the page.

   - Use lanes that are at roughly the same level of detail.

- Use job roles (instead of departments or functions) as lanes for less-complex work flows.

6. **Identify all of the process steps that occur between the triggering event and the outcome.**

   - Place the named process steps into boxes, and arrange them in sequence inside the lane where they occur.
   - Label each box using a "verb + [qualified] noun" format (e.g., "Find Available Contractors") or use a unique number to identify each box in sequence.
   - Illustrate decision points with diamonds.
   - Represent the triggering event as a right-facing arrow to the left of the first process box.
   - Represent the outcome as a left-facing arrow to the right of the last process box.

 Document business rules as text statements associated with process steps (instead of using a decision diamond) at each place where a business rule must be enforced (e.g., "Assign Contractor–The maximum number of jobs per individual contractor per day is five"). List documented business rules at the bottom of your process map.

7. **Identify the outputs of each step.**

   - Draw lines connecting the process boxes that provide outputs to other process boxes. Add an arrowhead, showing its direction into another process.
   - Label each line using high-level names (e.g., "Available Contractors" rather than individual data attributes such as "Contractor Name" or "Contractor Phone").

8. **Review the diagram and revise it as needed.**

   - Be sure that all of the steps are at roughly the same level of detail and that each step is necessary to produce the outcome.

Software Requirements

CVGC Process Map

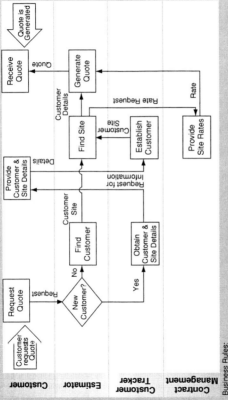

Customer

Request Quote ← Request

Customer requests Quote

Receive Quote ← Quote

Quote is Generated

Estimator

New Customer? → No / Yes

Find Customer

Provide Customer & Site Details → Details

Customer Site

Find Site

Generate Quote

Customer Details

Customer Tracker

Obtain Customer & Site Details

Request for Information

Establish Customer

Customer Site

Contract Management

Provide Site Rates → Rate

Rate Request

Business Rules:
"Generate Quote"—Existing customers receive a discounted rate.
"Receive Quote"—Quotes are valid for the fourteen days between quote-date and job scheduling date.

©2005 GOAL/QPC

Tip

Develop five or six scenarios (see section 4.7.4 for more information on scenarios) and walk each scenario through the process map to uncover missing steps, policies, or participants.

⫘ *Links to other models*

- Some process steps may represent one or more use cases or use case steps.

- Some processes may represent processes on a *data flow diagram*.

- A "to-be" process map roughly equates to a *use case map* (except that a use case map only includes automated processes).

- Inputs and outputs can become entities or attributes in the data model.

Variations

4.2.1 Identifying Manual Processes

Identify which steps in the business process will be manual. Have businesspeople identify manual documents and training that could be revised for any non-automated steps. Circle the leftover processes to show the scope of the software solution.

4.2.2 Automation Lanes

Draw the process map with an additional lane reserved for "automation" to illustrate those steps that require interfaces with software.

Understanding Project Scope

Defining which requirements are in scope reduces the biggest risk of software projects – scope creep (i.e., the unrestrained expansion of requirements as the project proceeds). Representations of scope-level requirements establish a common language for communicating about the requirements and help to articulate the boundary between what is in and what is out of the product.

A clear definition of product scope also narrows the project's focus to enable better planning, use of time, and use of resources. If the project scope is unclear, it is better to cancel or delay the project until the scope can be clarified and agreed to by the key stakeholders.

4.3 Context Diagram

What is it?

A context diagram shows the system in its environment, with the external entities (i.e., people and systems) that provide and receive information or materials to and from the system.

Alternative names for this model

- Scope Diagram

Why use it?

To help stakeholders quickly and simply define the project scope, and to focus on what the system needs as inputs and provides as outputs. The context diagram helps the team derive requirements models (e.g., actors, use cases, and data model information) and can surface possible scope creep problems as new external entities are added.

What does it do?

- Helps the team identify external stakeholders, systems, or subsystems that provide or receive system information or products.
- Allows the team to focus from the outside in, avoiding the tendency to jump into too much detail too soon
- Provides a starting point for understanding the data used by the system and fed to other systems or people
- Verifies the direct and indirect users identified in the stakeholder list

Key questions that this model will answer

- Who or what provides and receives information or products to and from the system?

- What does the system receive from entities outside the system?

How do I do it?

1. **Draw a circle to represent the system and label it with the system name.**

2. **Identify the external entities.**

   - Identify the people or things (e.g., other systems or physical devices) that get something from the system, or that give something to the system. Draw these external entities as boxes and label them.

   - Review the direct and indirect user names in the stakeholder list for possible external entities.

Tip A single external entity may give and get numerous things to and from the system.

3. **Add information flows.**

   - Draw a line with an arrowhead representing an information flow, query, or object (i.e., report, data, invoice, etc.) going into or out of the system, for each external entity.

   - Label the information flows, using an "adjective + noun" format (e.g., "Project Results Query," "Employee Identification Data," or "Order Details"); do not use verbs. Keep the information at a high level; do not list individual data elements going to or from the system.

   - Look for multiple input flows and external entities with similar labels; these may be the same thing

---

Software Requirements

and can be generalized into one label (e.g., entities such as "Distributor," "Supplies Distributor," or "E-business Distributor" with the same information flows on a diagram could be generalized into one external entity with the label "Distributor").

4. **After you draft other user requirements (such as the glossary, event-response table, actor table, and use cases), verify these models against the context diagram, revising them as necessary.**

• Involve sponsor(s), champions, and direct users (or their surrogates) in the review.

Ask stakeholders to use project goals and objectives to prioritize the criteria for what is in scope or out of scope and then rank sets of inflows and outflows using those criteria. If a project goal is to "Retain Contractors and Customers," less-important inputs or outputs such as "Supplies" can be removed or deferred for inclusion in a future release.

• Ensure that each inflow and corresponding outflow is necessary to achieve the project goals.

• Update the stakeholder list with any new direct users or indirect users.

• Define any new nouns on information flows in the glossary.

Expect to iteratively develop the context diagram. Input and output flows and external entities will evolve as you learn more about the requirements.

Supplement the context diagram with a list of external entities or information flows that are *not* in scope. This information may be in scope for a follow-up project that would enhance the initial release of the product.

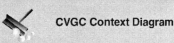

CVGC Context Diagram

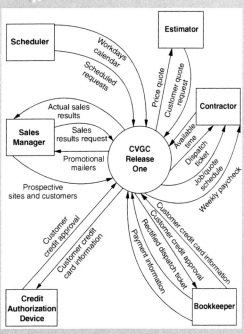

Scheduler

Workdays calendar

Scheduled requests

Estimator

Price quote

Customer quote request

Contractor

Actual sales results

Sales Manager

Sales results request

Promotional mailers

CVGC Release One

Available time

Dispatch ticket

Job/quote schedule

Weekly paycheck

Prospective sites and customers

Customer credit card information

Customer credit approval

Rectified dispatch ticket

Payment information

Customer credit approval

Customer credit card information

Credit Authorization Device

Bookkeeper

Software Requirements

A change in the context diagram implies a scope change, which may affect the project plan, completion dates, and project resources. Be sure that the project's sponsors, champions, and managers are aware of any such change and that requirements change-control processes are in place to handle these situations. (See Chapter 6 for more information on change-control processes.)

∞ Links to other models

- Inflows equate to business events in the event-response table.
- Outflows equate to responses in the event-response table (for responses that go beyond changing data internal to the system).
- Human external entities can become actors.
- Inflows can be associated with one or more use cases.
- Nouns on flow labels can become *data entities* or attributes in the data model.
- Nouns on inflows can become generalized names that are detailed in a *data dictionary*.

Variations

4.3.1 Vision Context Diagram

For large projects or ones in which the scope is unclear, create a separate "vision" context diagram that represents all of the "wish-list" external entities and information flows users would like to see included in the project. (Be sure to label it as a vision diagram.) Review the project goals and vision statements and then filter out the external entities and information flows on the vision context diagram that are not essential to the short-term achievement of the vision. Redraw the vision context diagram as the "to-be" system.

4.4 Event-Response Table

What is it?

An event-response table identifies each event (i.e., an input stimulus that triggers the system to carry out some function) and the event responses resulting from those functions.

Alternative names for this model

- Event Table
- Event List

Why use it?

To define all of the conditions to which the system must respond, thereby defining the functional requirements at a scope level. (Each event requires a predictable response from the system.) Creating an event-response table can also surface needs for external database access or file feeds.

What does it do?

- Clarifies the dynamics that drive system behavior
- Provides a starting point for identifying use cases
- Explains which events trigger outflows on a context diagram
- Helps the team identify possible scheduled or batch system jobs

Key questions that this model will answer

- When will the system perform tasks?
- What will the system response be?
- What things will happen automatically?

How do I do it?

1. **Name the events and classify them as business, temporal, or signal events.**

   • Name the business events using a "subject + verb + object" format (e.g., "Customer Requests Quote" or "Advertising Coordinator Queries Quarterly Sales"). Business events cause human users to initiate an interaction with the system. Business events are unpredictable with regard to frequency and timing, although their occurrence can be estimated based on past history.

   • Name the *temporal events* using a "time to <verb + object>" format (e.g., "Time to Generate Invoice" or "Time to Create Paychecks"). Temporal events are time-based triggers that originate when "the clock" says it is time to do something. These events trigger automatic system updates of internal files or the creation of system outputs such as reports, checks, bills, notification, or database feeds to other systems. Temporal events are completely predictable and will result in scheduled jobs or batch runs.

   • Name the *signal events* in a "subject + verb + object" format (e.g., "Traffic Sensor Detects Movement" or "Spinner Ejects Water"). Signal events originate from hardware devices.

   To uncover events of all types, ask, "What triggers the system to do something?" To uncover *business events*, ask, "What causes someone to interact with the system in some way?" To uncover *temporal events*, ask, "When does the system need to automatically generate something for people or for another system?" To uncover *signal events*, ask, "What indicators or stimuli do hardware devices generate that the system must respond to?"

- Have a draft glossary on-hand when listing events, and use the nouns consistently. Ask stakeholders to actively search for and correct confusing terms.

2. **For each event, describe its required response.**

   - Format event responses as "<object> provided to <subject>" or "system stores <information>." Include the production of some tangible item (e.g., a report, a record in a data file, or query result), the storage or change of the internal state of data, or some combination.

3. **Verify the event-response table against existing models and revise it as needed.**

   - Check the table against the context diagram to ensure that each inflow has a business event and that both models describe all responses. Keep the context diagram and event-response table in agreement with one another. Responses to temporal and signal events can generate outflows on the context diagram but they can also trigger internal system activities that are not visible on the context diagram (e.g., updating data or creating security or audit files). Similarly, business events may have no visible response on the context diagram, such as when the only system response is to store data.

   - Define, agree upon, and add any new nouns to the glossary.

CVGC Event-Response Table

Event	Event Type	Response
Estimator Provides Customer with Quote	Business	Quote provided to estimator; system stores quote information
Scheduler Sets Up Job	Business	Dispatch ticket provided to scheduled contractor; system stores schedule
Bookkeeper Reconciles Job	Business	System records customer payment; system generates contractor paycheck; system stores actual job information
Time to Generate Promotional Mailers	Temporal	Mailers sent to customer
Credit Authorization Device Signals Credit Disposition	Signal	System records authorization information

When software will be released incrementally, functional requirements that are associated with some rows on the event-response table may be implemented in future releases.

Be wary of finding *no* temporal events when replacing an existing automated system. These systems often contain automated feeds, reports, and outputs that need to be carried into the new system.

⚭ *Links to other models*

- Business events generate inflows on the context diagram.
- The "subject" in a business event name equates to an external entity on the context diagram and a direct user in the stakeholder list.

- The "object" in a business event name should be a noun in the glossary and part of the data model (or data dictionary).

- Temporal events may generate outflows on the context diagram.

- The "object" part of a temporal event name should be a noun in the glossary and data model.

- Event-responses can appear as flows on a context diagram and possibly data entities or attributes.

- The functionality needed to respond to events can be described with use cases.

- The "verb + object" parts of events provide a starting list of use cases, since use cases are named in a "verb + object" format (e.g., the business event "Customer Requests Quote" will evolve into the use case "Request Quote"; the temporal event "Time to Create Paychecks" will equate to the use case "Generate Paychecks"; and the signal event "Traffic Sensor Detects Movement" would evolve into the use case "Initiate Signal Change").

Variations

4.4.1 Additional Columns

Add optional columns to an event-response table to indicate event frequency (i.e., the number of times an event happens in a specific time frame), example data elements (i.e., pieces of data needed), or delivery method (e.g., interactive voice response, electronic feed, graphical interface, or fax).

4.4.2 Real-Time Systems

For real-time systems applications (i.e., systems that must respond to events within a predetermined time), re-

---

sponses include leaving the system in a specific state. Add an "end-state of the system" column to the event-response table for those types of systems. For example, for the signal event "Solution Temperature Exceeds Preset Level," the response might be "Notify Operator; Close Intake Valve," and the additional end-state column might be "Valve Set to Off; Solution-Mix Rate Set to Off." Adding this column can be beneficial for certain business systems, especially those that leave important data in a specific state.

4.5 Business Policies

What are they?

Business policies are the guidelines, standards, and regulations that guide or constrain the conduct of a business. Policies are the basis for the decision making and knowledge that are implemented in the software and in manual processes. Whether imposed by an outside agency or from within the company, organizations use policies to streamline operations, increase customer satisfaction and loyalty, reduce risk, improve revenue, and adhere to legal requirements (and thereby stay in business).

Alternative names for this model
- Regulations
- Legislation
- Standards

Why use it?

To identify policies allocated to businesspeople, which will allow the business community to prepare for software implementation by updating procedures, guidelines, training, forms, and other assets necessary to enforce the policies. Some policies will also be allocated to software for implementation.

Derivation of Business Policies and Rules

Policies allocated to software must be explicitly defined as business rules (see section 4.11 for more information on business rules) and must be included in the final software requirements specification. Business rules evolve from higher-level policies that, in turn, originate from business goals. Business policies guide decision making and exist to support the higher level business goals (e.g., streamlining operations, increasing customer satisfaction and loyalty, and increasing revenue). Policies originate either from inside an organization or from an external entity such as a governmental agency.

Business Rules, Policies, and Goals

Business Goal — Increase repeat business by 25%

Business Policies — Provide discounts to loyal customers

Business Rules — Loyal customers are those who have their windows cleaned two or more times a year.

If a loyal customer schedules a job, provide 15% discount to the total.

What do they do?

- Clarify what policies are in scope for enforcement in the project

- Enable businesspeople to rethink unnecessary or inefficient policies

- Help the team discover additional people who may need to be involved in requirements to define and approve policies

Key questions that this model will answer

- What standards, regulations, legislation, and principles govern our business?

- What policies must we enforce in our business processes? Which will be enforced in the software?

- What is the justification and reasoning for these policies?

- Do our policies support our project and business goals?

How do I do it?

1. **Identify groupings of business policies for the problem domain.**

   - Look at regulations, standard operating procedures, training manuals, maintenance guidelines, job aids, and system documentation. Be sure you review both external and internal sources of policies.

   - Be sure that policies align with one or more business goals or objectives.

   - Consult with knowledgeable businesspeople.

   - Group policies into like groups and name each group to include many related policies (e.g., "Job Pricing," "Tax Reporting," or "Contractor Billing").

- Check that the groups are not too high-level. Be clear in which group you will organize any given policy (e.g., decompose a policy group name of "Marketing" into "Customer Discounting," "Advertising," "Sales Incentives," and "Commissions").

2. **Determine where you will allocate the policies.**

   - Identify if each policy will be manually enforced or if it will be implemented in the software.

   - Have businesspeople revise documentation, job aids, training, procedures, and manuals for policies allocated to the business community.

   - Decompose policies that are allocated to the software into business rules. (See section 4.11 for more information on business rules.)

 Tip Some project teams will choose to begin identifying business rules and then associate them to business policies, rather than beginning with policies.

3. **Document policies that are in scope for the project.**

   - Document policies and uniquely label each policy.

   - Consider identifying candidate attributes such as owner, origin (e.g., regulation, procedures, etc.), source (e.g., legislation, person, document, etc.), volatility (i.e., frequency of change), and jurisdiction (i.e., roles or locations that might override the policy).

   - Select only those attributes that you are willing to track and that serve some useful purpose for the project.

Rule breaking is a form of rule making. Rethink each policy: Is it necessary? Does it promote the business goals? Can we clearly identify why the policy is needed? Can the policy be enforced in software? Adding or enforcing policies costs time and money, so make sure that there is a good business case for doing so!

 Businesspeople must be actively involved in defining business policies. Policies should not originate from technical staff unless they are domain experts. In any case, senior business-people (such as the sponsor or product champion) must approve and ratify policies. Consider appointing a "rule czar" from the business community whose responsibility is to resolve issues around policies. Give the rule czar the ultimate authority for defining conflicting policies, removing extraneous policies, and revising dysfunctional policies.

CVGC Business Policies for Software Enforcement

Policy Group	Policy Identifier	Policies	Owner	Sources
Discounting	BP-1	Provide discounts to senior citizens.	Jim Bean, Marketing Director	Pricing guidelines in Marketing/ Pricing folder (last updated Jan. 4)
	BP-2	Provide discounts to military personnel.		
	BP-3	Provide discounts to repeat customers.		
Job Scheduling	BP-5	Allow only one Contractor to be assigned to each time slot.	Jane Yi, Scheduler	Contractors and bookeepers
	BP-6	Schedule only requested Contractors, unless clients agree to other Contractors.		
	BP-7	Schedule Callback Jobs after Requested Jobs.		
	BP-8	Schedule Jobs within a week of request.		
Refunding	BP-10	Allow Contractors to decide if a dissatisfied customer will receive a refund or have their service repeated at no charge.	Carol Regal, Bookeeper	See Web site pages of competitors as a basis
	BP-11	Schedule the same Contractor to reclean.		

⌘ *Links to Other Models*

- Business terms used in policy text will become glossary entries.

- Policies will decompose into one or more business rule statements.

Variations

4.5.1 Rethink Business Policies

Use business visioning to rethink business rules. Ask businesspeople to write or tell stories or scenarios of a better future for conducting the business process. Have them describe what a typical business scenario would be like. Use the scenarios as the basis for finding business policies and for noting which policies are not used or are working against your business goals.

Adding Detail to User Requirements

Once your product scope is clear, you will need to analyze requirements in more detail. Use multiple models, weaving from one to another, to create a rich understanding of user needs. Because the models link together, compare one model to another to reveal defects.

Plan a sequence for creating the models that will show which models will best articulate needs. (The sequence, however, matters less than the act of iterating between the models to learn about the requirements and reveal requirements defects.) Begin by defining and analyzing one model, then switch to another, periodically returning to each model to detail or correct it.

4.6 Actor Table

What is it?

An actor table identifies and classifies system users in terms of their roles and responsibilities.

 Alternative names for this model
- Actor Catalog
- Actor Description
- User Role Model

Why use it?

To detect missing system users, to identify functional requirements such as user goals (use cases), and to help businesspeople clarify job responsibilities.

What does it do?
- Names and describes the human and nonhuman roles that interact with the system and the system-related responsibilities of those roles
- Describes the roles of direct users that interact with the system
- Supplements the actor map

 Key questions that this model will answer
- Who or what needs to interact with the system?
- What role or roles do they play when interacting with the system?
- What are the responsibilities for people or things that interact with the system?

Software Requirements

How do I do it?

1. **List the roles played in the system and place the role name in the "Actor" column of the table.**

   • Do not list actors as job titles or specific people. Instead, list them as abstractions of a job based on the actor's need to get something specific accomplished with the system. (Actors include people, other systems, hardware devices, and "the clock" or a timer.)

   • Draw upon the direct users from the stakeholder classes and the external entities on the context diagram.

    A direct user can play multiple roles, and a single actor can represent multiple people. For example, a Contractor, as shown on the context diagram, may be a "Service Provider," "Schedule Reviewer," and "Job Seeker." Conversely, the actor "Scheduler" may be played by multiple direct users, including the scheduler, the office manager, and the estimator.

    Name human actors with "-er" (e.g., "Window Cleaner," "Job Seeker," "Bookkeeper") or "-or" (e.g., "Contractor," "Paycheck Generator") words.

2. **Place attributes for each actor in additional columns.**

   • Write a brief description of each actor's responsibilities.

   • Add additional columns to hold other attributes (if necessary) such as:

      - Related job titles.

      - Location.

      - Names of actual people.

- Level of system usage expertise.

- Domain expertise.

- Frequency of use.

3. **Review the actor table for missing or extraneous actors.**

- Involve stakeholders such as sponsors, champions, and direct users (or their surrogates) in the review.

- Be sure each direct user (from the stakeholder categories) and each external entity (from the context diagram) is described as one or more actors.

- Explore the possibility that other stakeholders such as advisors or providers might also be actors.

- Look for additional nonhuman actors such as other systems and hardware devices that help actors accomplish tasks.

- Check actors against events in the event-response table. (The event-response table should include actors (or pseudo-actors) that either initiate system interactions when events occur or receive system responses as a result of events.)

- Add any newly discovered actors to the actor table.

- Update the context diagram with any new external entities discovered while identifying actors.

CVGC Actor Table

Actor	Attributes and Responsibilities	Job Title(s)
Scheduler	Find available Contractors for a Customer's request that match the location. Arrange for services by Contractors at Customer location on requested days and times.	Scheduler, Office Manager
Job Closer	Reconcile Estimated and Scheduled Jobs with Completed Jobs. Apply payments. Issue invoices for Completed but Unpaid Jobs. Update Customer details for changes in site conditions.	Bookkeeper, Office Manager, Scheduler
Bookkeeper	Generate daily or weekly paychecks to Contractors and ensure that all taxes are properly deducted. Post payments (delivered by Contractors or received directly from Customers via credit card or check). Ensure that all Accounts Payable and Receivables are balanced.	Bookkeeper
Service Provider	Travel to Customer's location, clean windows, and provide related services such as power-washing decks and gutter cleaning. Serve Customers, take payments by cash or check, and provide Customers with invoices on-site of the actual work performed. Occasionally estimate Jobs. Bid on open Jobs and maintain personal information. Most Service Providers are independent Contractors.	Contractor

Tip During design, extend the actor table to record allowable database access rules for each actor (e.g., create-read-update-delete (CRUD) rights by data entity).

Tip Creating higher level actor names with specializations can slim-down user requirements by reducing redundancy in describing user tasks. Each next-level actor performs essentially the same tasks, with some differences in the specific data he or she can access or the business rules he or she can enforce.

Variations

4.6.1 Actor Map

Use an actor map (also referred to as an actor hierarchy or user role model) to show actor interrelationships. An actor map supplements the actor table and can also be used as a starting point for identifying use cases. Actors can be written on index cards (one per index card) or drawn using the *Unified Modeling Language (UML)* notation. The UML notation depicts actors in an actor map as all stick figures, as all boxes (supplemented by the notation "<<Actor>>"), or as a combination (e.g., stick figures for human actors and boxes for nonhuman actors). Be consistent in notation across all actor maps.

Arrange actors as *specialization, aggregation* (similar to composition), or both. Specializations show specific roles as variants of a more common, abstract role. Show specializations as a hierarchy using lines with open arrowheads pointing toward the common role at the top of the hierarchy. For additional clarity, add, "<<specialize>>" on the line. Aggregation illustrates a group assembly; in this usage, showing how a role is comprised of (includes) other roles. Show aggregation with the aggregated role above the included roles, combined with the diamond.

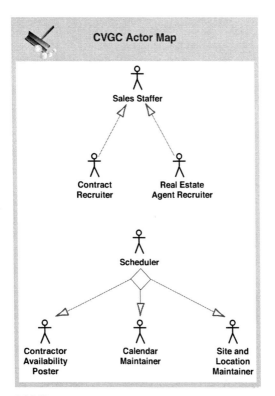

CVGC Actor Map

Sales Staffer

Contract Recruiter

Real Estate Agent Recruiter

Scheduler

Contractor Availability Poster

Calendar Maintainer

Site and Location Maintainer

4.6.2 Personas

Personas describe actors as fictional system users or archetypes. Describe each persona as if he or she is a real person with a personality, family, work background, preferences, behavior patterns, and personal attitudes. Focus on behavior patterns rather than job descriptions.

Write each persona description as a narrative flow of the person's day, with added details about personality. Invent four or five personas to represent the roles that use the system most often or are most important to the functional requirements.

Links to other models

- Actors are roles played by direct users (from the stakeholder categories).

- External entities on the context diagram can also be actors.

- Actor names and their qualifiers are candidate glossary entries.

- Actor name qualifiers can also be candidate data attributes (in the data model) or data entries (in the data dictionary).

- Actors can trigger events, perhaps with participation by other actors.

- Actors initiate use cases.

4.7   Use Cases

What are they?

Use cases are descriptions in abstract terms of how actors use the system to accomplish goals. Each use case is a logical piece of user functionality that can be initiated by an actor and described from the actor's point of view in a technology-neutral manner. A use case summarizes a set of related scenarios.

 ### Alternative names for this model

- Task

- Script

- Use Case Specification

Why use them?

To reveal functional requirements by clarifying what users need to accomplish when interacting with the system. Use cases are a natural way to organize functional requirements and can be easier for users to understand and verify than textual functional requirements statements.

What do they do?

- Specify user requirements as actor goals that are described as sequences of interactions between the actor and the system
- Document detailed steps for normal system usage as well as for handling errors and variations
- Help discover business rules and necessary data
- Provide easy-to-read requirements documentation for users who cannot participate in face-to-face requirements elicitation
- Provide a shorthand way to discuss sets of related scenarios
- Group user requirements in a manner that facilitates requirements prioritization and determining incremental software releases
- Provide a basis for developing test cases

What does a use case include?

Use cases can be defined in text, diagrams, or both.

A textual use case has five parts:

1. A header that provides high-level identification information about the use case.

2. A brief description that summarizes what the use case accomplishes.

3. Detailed steps that the actor and system go through to accomplish the use case goal.

4. Exceptions that describe the steps for handling errors and exceptions.

5. Variations that describe the steps for handling alternative courses through each use case.

Note: It is important to identify requirements information (such as the use-case initiating actor, needed data, and business rules) for related models at the same time.

You do not need to write every use case with the same level of detail. For simple use cases, the header and brief description are usually sufficient.

? *Key questions that this model will answer*

- What goals do actors have?
- What steps (or tasks) are involved in accomplishing each use case goal?
- What must happen to respond to each event?
- What steps occur in multiple use cases?
- What could go wrong at each step?
- What might interrupt any given step?

How do I do it?

1. **Create an initial list of use cases.**

   - Select one actor at a time, and name the use case as a goal the actor accomplishes by interacting with the system. Name each use case with an "active verb + [qualifier] noun" format (e.g., "Pay Contractors" or "Close Out Job"). Avoid passive names (i.e., "Job is Scheduled" is passive; "Schedule Job" is active). Also avoid vague verbs (such as "Do," "Process," or "Maintain") in naming use cases.

   - Include use cases that respond to temporal events (e.g., "Archive Inactive Customers" and "Generate Discount Mailers"). These use cases primarily change data in the system or generate outputs.

   - Use the guideline "more is better" in the early steps of defining use cases. If multiple related actor goals emerge, separate them rather than combine them. For example, use cases that establish data and those that modify that same data are related, but "Set Up Contractor Profiles" and "Modify Contractor Profile" should be kept separate at this point. (They may become a single use case with multiple variations on a common theme later in analysis).

CVGC Initial List of Use Cases

Schedule Job	Provide Phone Estimate
Estimate Job	Dispatch Job
Pay Contractor	Search for Jobs
Review Job Schedule	Close Out Job
Send Mailers	Define Geographic Areas
Authorize Customer Credit	Grant User Permission
Record Callback Details	Set Up Company
Modify Company Details	Set Up Pricing Speci-
Adjust Pricing Speci-	fications
fications	Post Payment
Set Up Contractor Profiles	Define County and State
Generate 1099s for IRS	Taxes
Set Up Customer	Review Cancelled and
Find Available Contractor	Rescheduled Jobs
Search Schedule	Pay for Job

- Include use cases that authenticate users and administer access rights.

Tip Business users don't think about database actions when they interact with the system, so avoid fine-grained CRUD use cases such as "Create Customer" or "Update Address." These are specific steps that will occur in the context of a higher actor goal.

Tip Identify use cases using a top-down, bottom-up, or middle-out approach. In a top-down approach, develop use cases from requirements scope or business models. For example:

- Using a context diagram, ask, "What goals are accomplished by the system handling each of these external entities?"

- For each event in an event-response table, ask, "What goal is triggered by this event?"

- Using a process map or a relationship map, ask, "What actions does the system do to accomplish this process or transform the inputs and outputs?"

In a middle-out approach, develop use cases by naming the actor goals. In a bottom-up approach, group and label scenarios by their common theme by asking, "What do these scenarios have in common?"

Tip Use cases tend to be either *informative*—providing information to actors (suggesting such verbs as "List," "View," "Notify," "Access," and "Query")—or *performative*—allowing actors to handle complex tasks (suggesting such verbs as "Prepare," "Schedule," "Assign," "Evaluate," and "Configure"). Refer to the verbs suggested in Appendix C of this book to describe informative and performative use cases.

2. **Create a brief description for each use case.**

- Write several sentences describing what the use case accomplishes. Write your description abstractly enough so that multiple audiences (e.g., customers, users, and technical people) will understand it.

- Avoid long lists of data. Include data needed by the use case in the data model.

Tip Remove business rule statements from the use case text. Business rules operate across use cases. Define them separately and include a cross-reference to business rules from use cases.

---

3. Create a header for each use case.

Use Case Header	Explanation
Use Case Identification Number	Unique use case number
Use Case Name	Name of the use case, in verb-object format, that describes the actor's goal
Preconditions	List of preceding use cases, state of the system before the use case can proceed, or both
Post-Conditions (or Success Outcome)	State of the system after successful completion
Primary Actor	The actor that initiates the use case and interacts with the system to accomplish the goal
Secondary Actor(s)	Supporting actor(s) needed by the system to complete the use case
Triggering Event	Business, temporal, or signal event that causes the actor to initiate the use case

You can document preconditions in several ways. Document a *preceding use case* in a work-flow approach. For systems with complex and discrete states (e.g., claim adjudication, network trafficking, engine ignition), document the state of the system before the use case can start. Also add system state information to the precondition (e.g., "Job is in an 'Entered' State" or "Engine is 'Idle'").

Post-conditions describe the use case outcome, assuming it has been successfully completed. This is analogous to the response column of the event-response table.

- Update any use case diagrams to include *secondary actors*. Add secondary actors to the actor table and actor map, if used.

4. **Verify the initial set of use cases before adding details to each.**

   - Make sure each use case is necessary to achieve your business goals and has at least one initiating actor.
   - Make sure that each actor initiates (or is a secondary actor in) at least one use case. If this does not occur, identify any missing use cases or remove any extraneous actors.

CVGC Use Case Header and Brief Description for the Use Case "Pay Contractors"

Header

Use Case ID Number: UC16

Use Case Name: Pay Contractors

Primary Actor: Paycheck Generator

Secondary Actor: Payroll System

Triggering Event: Contractor Completes Work Order

Preconditions: Use Case 1 (Authenticate User), Use Case 3 (Reconcile Job); The Contractor is "active"

Post-Conditions: A check is generated and the payment is posted to the Payroll System

Brief Description

Compute all line items for each completed job and produce a check. The system stores reconciled job information and payment details.

5. Determine the steps in the use case.

- List each step that the actor and system must do to achieve a goal.

- Write the steps in either sequential form (i.e., one step per line) or conversational form (i.e., two columns: one for the actor and one for the system).

 CVGC Use Case Basic Flow: Sequential Format

Use Case: Search Schedule

1. Schedule Reviewer requests schedule for specific day.

2. System provides list of companies and contractors from which to select.

3. Schedule Reviewer selects a contractor.

4. System provides scheduled jobs in sequential order.

5. Schedule Reviewer selects a specific job from the schedule.

6. System displays details about customer, location, and requested services.

**CVGC Use Case
Main Sequence:
Conversational Format**

Use Case: Search Schedule

Actor Action	System Response
1. Request schedule for specific day.	2. Display list of companies and contractors.
3. Select contractor.	4. Display scheduled jobs in sequence.
5. Select specific job.	6. Display details about customer, location, and requested services.

Tip

Other names for steps in a use case include "basic flow," "normal flow," "happy path," or "basic course of events."

- Keep the step descriptions general. Avoid long lists of data attributes (e.g., write "Select a Specific Location for a Site" instead of "Search for Location Code using Site Identifier").

- Do not list steps that handle errors or unusual situations in the basic flow. Document these errors or situations separately in an "exceptions" section. (See step 7 for more information on exceptions.)

- Indicate if the specific sequence of steps is required by adding "In the following order" at the beginning of the steps. (Otherwise, the step order is a guideline.)

- If you are using the conversational format, add a third column when actors interact with a combination of the system and people. For example, a checkout use case for a store's point-of-sales system can include the customer actor, the clerk, and the point-of-sales device.

 Avoid text such as "If ...Then...Else" in the text of the basic flow, exceptions, and alternatives. "If" conditions often indicate business rules. Review each step to uncover any business rules that constrain action (e.g., "Only one Contractor is assigned to a Job") or enable action (e.g., "When Job rescheduling is needed for reasons other than customer request, offer 10% discount"). Move these to the business rules document.

6. **Test the steps for sequence and completeness.**

   - Check that the order of each step represents the common flow of events needed to achieve the actor's goal.

   - Be sure that you did not miss any steps.

 To efficiently test use cases, document scenarios of normal system use and walk through each step in the use case. Be sure the use case steps describe what must happen in sufficiently abstract terms to encompass all related scenarios.

7. **Determine the steps for use case exceptions.**

   - Document exception steps (i.e., interruptions of the basic flow that result in not achieving the use case post-conditions) below the basic flow in an "exceptions" section.

   - Label each step beginning with the step number from the basic flow where the error occurs and follow it by a period and substep number. If there are two possible and mutually exclusive exceptions to a step, number them in sequence (e.g., 2.1 and 2.2)

   - Add letters to the label if multiple actions can occur within substeps (e.g., 3.1a, 3.1b).

CVGC Use Case Exception

HEADER: <header follows>
BRIEF DESCRIPTION: <brief description follows>
BASIC FLOW: <basic flow follows>
EXCEPTIONS:

3	Schedule Reviewer selects a non-active Contractor.
3.1a	System asks Schedule Reviewer if she wants to cancel the request or select another Contractor.
3.1b	Schedule Reviewer cancels request
3.1c	System terminates use case.

8. **Document steps for any use case variations.**

   • Document variations steps (i.e., branches, optional ways, or alternative ways to accomplish the use case goal while still meeting the use case post-conditions) below the exceptions in a "variations" section.

   • Consider situations that occur infrequently (e.g., selecting a schedule for a week vs. a day) or optionally (e.g., making a direct deposit to a contractor's banking account rather than generating a paycheck).

   • Label each step beginning with the step number from the basic flow, followed by a period and substep number. If there are two possible and mutually exclusive variations to a step, number them in sequence (e.g., 2.1 and 2.2).

   • Add letters to the label if multiple actions can occur (e.g., 2.1a).

CVGC Use Case Variations

HEADER: <header follows>
BRIEF DESCRIPTION: <brief description follows>
BASIC FLOW: <basic flow follows>
EXCEPTIONS: <exception flow follows>
VARIATIONS:

1	Schedule Reviewer requests schedule for more than one day.
1.1a	System asks Schedule Reviewer for range of days or weeks.
1.1b	Schedule Reviewer provides time frame for the query.
1.1c	System proceeds with step 2 in basic flow.

9. **Identify and separately document** *included use cases.*

   • Document any included use case (i.e., a common set of steps used in multiple use cases) in the same manner as any other use case—with a header, a brief description, a basic flow, exceptions, and variations. (A use case can incorporate the steps that comprise another (included) use case.)

   • In the header of the included use case, document the use cases that incorporate it in the "trigger" portion, in place of a triggering event.

   • In the header of the incorporating use case, document included use cases by adding "Includes <included use case numbers>."

   • In the body of the invoking use case (i.e., the use case that uses the included use case), underline the names of any included use cases or insert the included use case name in carets (e.g., "<included use case name>").

10. Check use cases for missing requirements.

- Ensure that each event is associated with at least one use case, and update the event-response table, if needed.

- Ensure that each primary actor initiates at least one use case.

- Consider adding a column in the actor table naming the use cases that each actor initiates.

- Document each business rule that a use case must enforce in the business rules document.

- Document data attributes that each use case must access or store in the data model.

11. Define attributes to associate to use cases.

- Place associated attributes (e.g., owner, priority, planned release, complexity, and dependencies) in a section of the use case or in a separate matrix, using one row per use case.

Ask questions to elicit related quality attributes, such as "What is the maximum response time acceptable for <use case>?" "How often will <use case> be used?" "Will the frequency vary in different locations?" "Are there periods of higher volume?" and "Will experienced and new users need to learn to use this functionality differently?" These provide clues to quality attributes that need to be included in the software requirements specification.

CVGC Use Case Attributes

Use Case ID	Use Case Name	Dependencies	Business Owner	Priority	Planned Release	Complexity
UC1	Grant User Permission	–	Paul Deer	Mandatory	1	Low
UC3	Estimate Job	UC1	Jane Yi	Mandatory	1	High
UC5	Schedule Job	UC3, UC1	Jane Yi	Mandatory	1	High
UC7	Adjust Pricing Specifications	UC8	Jim Bean	Optional	3	Low
UC8	Define Geographic Areas	UC10	Jim Bean	Important	2	Low
UC9	Close Out Job	UC5	Carol Regal	Mandatory	1	Medium

CVGC Full Use Case

Use Case ID Number:	UC5
Use Case Name:	Schedule Job
Primary Actor:	Scheduler
Secondary Actor:	n/a
Triggering Event:	Scheduler sets up job
Includes:	Use Case 5 (Find Available Contractors); Use Case 2 (Estimate Job)
Preconditions:	Customer is "Active"; Scheduler is logged into the System
Post-conditions:	Job information is stored in the System; Dispatch ticket is issued to the scheduled Contractor

Brief Description:
The Scheduler uses the information from the Customer to search for available Contractors for the requested time and services. An estimate of the Job is provided, the Contractor is scheduled, and a dispatch ticket is provided to the scheduled Contractor.

Basic Flow:
1. Scheduler requests services for the requested date and customer location.
2. System <Find Available Contractors>.
3. System displays available contractors.
4. Scheduler selects a contractor.
5. System <Estimate Job>.
6. System displays estimate.
7. System provides the scheduled date and time for the selected contractor.
8. Scheduler accepts that estimate and schedule.
9. System generates dispatch ticket for the contractor.

Continued on next page

CVGC Full Use Case

Exceptions:

3.   No contractors are available for the requested date or time.
3.1a System asks scheduler if she wants to cancel the request or select another date.
3.1b Scheduler cancels request.
3.2a Scheduler asks for another date.
3.2b System proceeds with step 1 in basic flow with new dates.

Variations:

1.   Scheduler requests schedule options for more than one day.
1.1   System asks scheduler to provide range of days or weeks or specific days within a two-week period.
1.2   Scheduler provides range of dates or specific days.
1.3   System proceeds with step 2 in basic flow.

Document use cases in the "essential" form (i.e., devoid of any technology or design assumptions). Do not include user interface design information (i.e., remove words such as "window," "click," and "button"). Place related quality attributes, such as response time, reliability, and number of concurrent users, in use case documentation, matrices, or your software requirements specification.

Be sure to choose models that best express the requirements. Not all user requirements fit the use case technique. For example, domains that query and report information are best represented with combinations such as a data model, business rules, and user questions. Requirements for real-time software are rarely a fit for use cases.

⚙ *Links to other models*

- Each part of a textual use case—header, brief description, steps, exceptions, and variations—requires associated business rules.

- Nouns in use case steps refer to data in the data model.

- Use case steps describe a set of related scenarios.

Variations

4.7.1 Use Case Diagram

Create a use case diagram to depict an "inside" view of the context diagram, showing pieces of system-scope functionality. Use case diagrams using UML notation represent the use case as an oval, labeled with the use case name and connected to its actors. (Actors include the primary or initiating actor and any participating or secondary actors.)

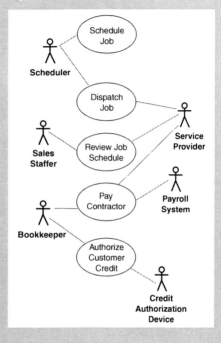

CVGC Use Case Diagram
Using UML Notation

Schedule
Job

Scheduler

Dispatch
Job

Sales
Staffer

Review Job
Schedule

Service
Provider

Pay
Contractor

Payroll
System

Bookkeeper

Authorize
Customer
Credit

Credit
Authorization
Device

Diagram use cases that respond to "clock" actors (i.e., those triggered by a device or temporal event) as an option. Invent pseudo-actor names such as "Payroll Controller" for an actor that initiates a use case by the event "Time to Produce 1099 Forms."

It is more important to have well-named use cases, with clear and concise descriptions, than to have use case diagrams.

4.7.2 Use Case Map

Illustrate the work flow of use cases by arranging them into chronological sequence with a use case map. Each use case map represents a set of highly cohesive use cases sharing the same data, often triggered by the same events or initiated by the same actor.

If two use cases can occur simultaneously, place one above the other, with the preceding use case to their left. Draw lines connecting the use case with arrowheads pointing to the right in sequence.

Conduct walk-throughs of the use case maps. Begin with a single event (or scenario) and step through the use cases in the map, looking for sequence errors. Look for missing requirements such as use cases, events, actors, or scenarios.

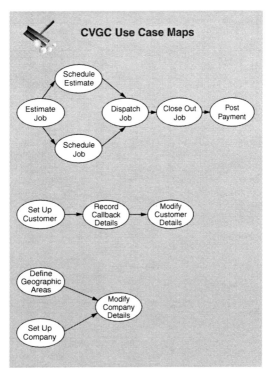

CVGC Use Case Maps

- Estimate Job
  - Schedule Estimate
  - Schedule Job
- Dispatch Job
- Close Out Job
- Post Payment

- Set Up Customer
- Record Callback Details
- Modify Customer Details

- Define Geographic Areas
- Set Up Company
- Modify Company Details

Tip Have testers employ use case maps to organize test plans and cases, and revise training materials and user documentation as necessary.

4.7.3 Use Case Packages

Derive *use case packages* (i.e., logical, cohesive groups of use cases that represent higher level system functionality) by combining use case maps or grouping use cases. Determine which use cases satisfy higher level functionality. (Most systems will have multiple packages.) You can use a UML file folder notation to show each package. Name each package according to its functionality. Document the use cases or use case map in the package.

Determine dependencies among packages by asking whether one package can operate without another package. If it cannot, it is dependent on other packages. Draw dependencies by connecting lines with arrowheads between packages. A package is *dependent upon* the package it points into.

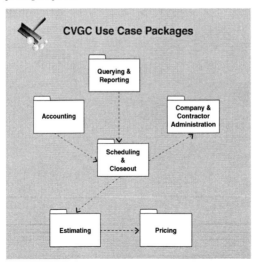

Have stakeholders prioritize each package, then group highly dependent and higher priority packages into software releases.

Use case packages show the logical architecture of system functionality. Designers can analyze packages to allocate functionality to hardware devices, subsystems, or systems software.

4.7.4 Scenarios

Scenarios can describe a specific occurrence of a path through a use case (i.e., a use case instance.)

**CVGC Scenario
for "Reschedule Job"**

"A customer calls to reschedule a job, adding another service and requesting a repeat customer discount."

You can also write detailed scenarios that reference specific data, and document that data in a table.

**CVGC Detailed Scenario
in a Table Format
with Attributes and Values
for "Use Case 5 – Schedule Job"**

Data Attributes	Data Values
Customer Name	Ian Arby
Scheduled Contractor	Jane Walker
Scheduled Date	Friday, June 7
Scheduled Time	10:00 a.m.
Payment Method	Credit
Reschedule Request Date	Friday, June 14
Reschedule Request Time	3:00 p.m.
Rescheduled Contractor	Mary Gordon
Service Adding	Mirror Clean
Service Adding Count	2
Re-estimated Amount	$210

Tip   Other team members such as testers and end-user acceptance testers can use scenarios to develop test cases and test scripts.

Tip   An alternative to writing detailed use cases is to name use cases, write the header and brief description, and then document scenarios for each use case to gain an overall understanding of requirements, without having to write detailed use cases. This also works when developers are knowledgeable about the domain.

4.7.5 Stories

Stories are text descriptions of a path through a use case that users typically document. Stories replace use cases and scenarios in planning releases for change-driven software projects. (See section 8.2 for more information on change-driven projects.) Stories are essentially the same as detailed scenarios, but each story is judged by developers to require less than two weeks to develop. When combined with acceptance tests, stories are roughly equivalent to use cases.

CVGC Story

"On Friday, June 7, Harry Feat leaves a message that he wants to reschedule the cleaning scheduled for Monday, June 10, and he wants to add two inside mirror cleanings to the job. He requests a phone estimate and the repeat customer discount. We tell him it will cost $250 after the 10% discount. We give him the next available day (the following Friday at 3:00 p.m.) with the same cleaner (Jim Dandy) that he had six months ago. He asks for an earlier date, and we give him Wednesday with another contractor (Elaine Mays) at 10 a.m. We confirm that he'll pay by credit card at the time of service, and we read back his credit card number to him on the phone."

4.7.6 Activity Diagram of a Use Case

An *activity diagram* illustrates the flow of complex use cases using UML notation. It is useful for showing the use case steps that have multiple extension steps, and for visualizing use cases.

Each rounded box represents a use case step. Branches from the main flow illustrate exceptions. The heavy bar synchronizes steps that come together before or after steps occur. The diagram can be drawn left-to-right or top-down. Swimlanes can also be added, showing rows for the actor and system.

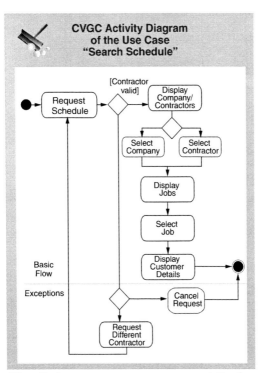

CVGC Activity Diagram of the Use Case "Search Schedule"

Alternatively, you can use a process map notation (see section 4.2) or a flowchart (drawn sideways rather than top to bottom) to diagram a use case.

4.7.7 Data Flow Diagram

A data flow diagram (DFD) models related inputs, processes, and outputs. It shows the processes that respond to an external or temporal event. Unlike use cases (which are oriented toward actor goals), DFDs focus on the data that goes in and out of each process, taking an internal view of how the system handles events.

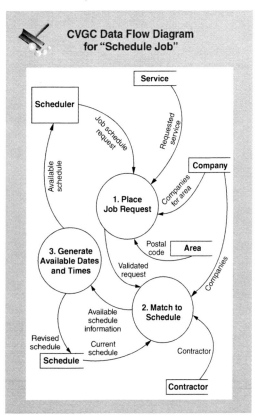

CVGC Data Flow Diagram
for "Schedule Job"

Data stores on a DFD roughly equate to data entities or structures in a data dictionary (which list attributes of a grouping of information). Each process transforms information by applying business rules (documented separately). Data flows represent one or more pieces of data used as input to or output from a process.

4.8   Dialog Map

What is it?

A *dialog map* is one or more visual diagrams that illustrate the architecture of the system's user interface. The dialog map shows visual elements that users manipulate to step through tasks when interacting with the system.

Alternative names for this model

- Context Navigation Map
- Storyboard
- User Interface Flow Diagram
- User Interface Navigation Diagram

Why use it?

To explore how users navigate through the system to accomplish tasks, to uncover missing or erroneous use case paths, and to validate use cases, scenarios, or both in requirements walk-throughs with users.

What does it do?

- Represents the user interface at a high level of abstraction
- Shows dialogs (i.e., windows, menus, work spaces, screens, prompts, text lines, and other visual or tactile elements) that end users can access
- Depicts interface paths through one or more use cases

- Illustrates how users move from one context to another and documents how transitions are triggered

- Provides a basis for constructing test cases to execute each possible navigation path

 Key questions that this model will answer

- What interface elements are available for direct users to see, touch, or otherwise control?

- How does a user navigate from dialog to dialog?

- What choices does the user have when using a specific dialog?

How do I do it?

1. **Select a single complex use case or a set of related use cases.**

   - Find a use case with multiple exception paths that are not well understood, or choose use cases from a use case map that pose concerns regarding meeting complex user needs or that may have missing user steps.

2. **Choose dialogs and identify transitions among them.**

   - Identify dialogs (i.e., actions or tasks that occur within the use case) and represent each dialog as a box.

   - Label each dialog box descriptively as a noun or qualified nouns.

   - Identify transitions from one dialog to another, including user-generated and system-generated triggers. Use action verbs (such as "Request," "Select," "Ask," "Cancel," and "Return") for user-generated triggers. Show system-generated triggers, including errors (such as "Invalid Data" or "No Match for User Selections"), as transitions to a dialog box labeled "Error Message."

Software Requirements

3. **Draw the diagram using the appropriate symbols and transition labels.**

   - Draw each transition between dialog boxes.
   - Add an arrowhead pointing to the dialog into which the transition occurs.
   - Label each transition with the user-generated or system-generated trigger.

4. **Verify the dialog map for completeness, correctness, and consistency.**

   - Be sure each transition is described in use case text.
   - Check that the dialog map depicts all navigation paths in a use case's basic flow (as well as exception and variation steps).
   - Correct any unreachable or inconsistent navigation paths.
   - Be sure that there are scenarios that elaborate on the flow of tasks shown in the dialog map.
   - Encourage testers to build test cases from the dialog map and use case text.

CVGC Dialog Map for the Use Case "Estimate Job"

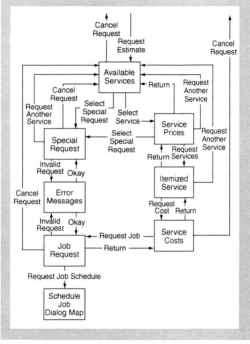

⬭ *Links to other models*

- Dialog boxes represent one or more steps in a use case.
- Transitions among dialog boxes depict a specific path through a use case.
- Scenarios involving user interfaces can be traced through navigation paths in the diagram.

Variations

4.8.1 Prototype

Build a low-fidelity prototype to show potential screen flows. (See section 3.4.3 for more information on prototypes.)

4.8.2 *Dialog Hierarchy*

To show the overall architecture of Web pages, arrange dialogs as a hierarchy, but do not show transitions.

CVGC Dialog Hierarchy

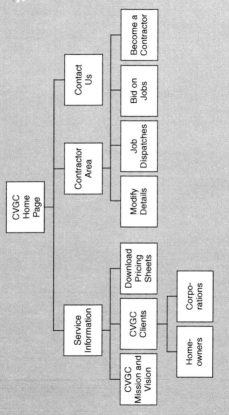

Software Requirements

4.9   Data Model

What is it?

A data model shows the informational needs of the system by illustrating the logical structure of data independent of the data design or data storage mechanism.

Alternative names for this model

- Conceptual Data Model
- Entity Relationship Diagram (ERD)
- Logical Data Model
- Domain Model

Why use it?

To identify, summarize, and formalize the data attributes and structures needed to satisfy functional requirements and to create an easy-to-maintain database. Data models help to simplify design and programming, and help identify external data entities (i.e., other systems that supply data to the software).

What does it do?

- Identifies the information groups to store and the relationships among them in a technology-neutral manner
- Illustrates the structure of the data after business rules have been enforced
- Eliminates redundant data and complex data structures
- Specifies rules to maintain data integrity
- Facilitates database design

Key questions that this model will answer

- What data do users need to access or save?
- What data is needed to enforce business rules?
- How will information be structured when all of the business rules are enforced?
- What constraints exist when records are added and deleted?

What is the data model used for?

The data model is the foundation for designing the physical data structures (i.e., tables and rows).

There are various notations and terminology standards for data modeling. The notations described in the table on the next page are example notations. For your project, use your company's, department's, or project's notation and naming standards.

Use the data model, data-related quality attributes, database management system (DBMS), and hardware capabilities to design your physical database. Data-related quality attributes include security (i.e., who can access what data), integrity (i.e., ensuring that the data can be recovered if there is a system failure), and performance needs such as response time and throughput (i.e., the amount of data expected to be accessed and the type of access needed).

The physical database design prepares the data for storage and access on disks. It includes access details such as data access paths, indices, and physical space calculations for optimal performance.

Data Model Building Blocks

Element	Explanation	Examples	Graphical Representation	Text Representation
Entities (nouns)	Things that indicate which data is stored. Entities can be people, places, or concepts (tangible or in-tangible, long-lived or short-lived).	Customer, Job, Site, Contractor, Location	Box (or a rounded box, depending on notation) Contractor	Name of the entity, often capitalized
Relationships (verbs)	Facts about entities or the connections among them. Each relationship is expressed in natural language, with a verb connecting the two entities.	Customer owns Account, Contractor services Job	Line connecting entity boxes and a verb on the connection line Contractor — is serviced by — services — Job	Entity <verb> Entity
Attributes (nouns)	Atomic information describing an entity. An attribute cannot be decomposed into smaller pieces without losing its meaning.	First name, service name, service cost, rate per hour, postal code, service date	Listed inside or outside an entity box Contractor — Contractor last name - character (15) Contractor first name - character (10) Contractor postal code - numeric (10) Contractor effective date - date (yy/mm/dd)	Text name, possibly supplemented with the size and format of the data

How do I do it?

1. Identify and define data entities.

- Think of entities as larger "things" to which you will add "thingettes" (attributes).

 Entities are nouns that you can describe with more than one attribute. Each entity represents a group of related information to be stored by the system such as people, roles, places, things, organizations, occurrences in time, and documents.

- Review the glossary for nouns that may be entities.

- Group related attributes into entities so that each entity shares common definitions and properties. For example, specific people (e.g., Jimmy Bob Devlin, Sally Ray, and Jerry Dunn) all belong to the same entity – "Contractor." All members or occurrences of the entity Contractor have the same generic definition and the same attributes (e.g., first and last name, phone number, and mailing address).

- Capitalize each entity and name it in the singular, referring to only one instance of it (i.e., "Contractor," not "Contractors").

- Draw each entity as a box with its name inside.

- Write a brief description of each entity or use one from the glossary, if available.

- List candidate attributes for each entity by asking, "What information do we need to keep about this entity?" or "What data do we keep about this entity?" Write the candidate attributes inside the box.

 Name specific examples of each entity. Make sure the definition fits each example. Each entity should have multiple examples.

 Alternatively, you can use a bottom-up approach that begins by naming attributes and then grouping them into entities. To do this, consider tangible outputs (e.g., reports, forms, invoices, signals, and potential user dialogs), list the attributes needed to produce them, and then group those that logically belong together. If you have use cases or scenarios, find nouns that may be attributes and group similar ones together.

2. **Define a primary key for each entity.**

   • Add the primary key to the diagram by writing the key at the top of the attribute list and underlining it, or by denoting it with "PK" (primary key) inside the entity box. To identify the primary key, ask, "What distinguishes instances of this entity from other occurrences of the same entity?"

The primary key is an attribute or minimal set of attributes that uniquely identifies an occurrence of each entity and must exist for every such occurrence. System-generated primary keys are unique numbers assigned by the system (e.g., Contractor ID or Job Number). Externally defined keys originate from an outside party (e.g., Postal Code, State, or Social Security Number).

Consult with the data administrator or database administrator for naming conventions. Do not abbreviate attributes or primary keys—use the full business names, but do abbreviate common words such as "Date" or "Amount." Share these abbreviations with businesspeople, and use them consistently in the data model.

3. **Identify relationships among the entities.**

   • To determine whether two entities should be related, ask, "Can <Entity Name> exist without <Entity Name>?" (e.g., "Can a Job exist without a related Contractor?"), then fill in the verb ("Contractor services Job").

- Draw a line connecting the related entities, and write the relationship rule (verb) on the line. Place the verb above the connecting line. Then rewrite the relationship in the passive voice (i.e., "Job is serviced by Contractor"), and place this below the connecting line.

 Tip Use descriptive verbs to identify the associations between entities, using the format "Entity <verb> Entity" (e.g., "Contractor services Job" or "Client is solicited by Callbacks"). (Avoid using the verb "has.") Each verb describes a relationship rule and explains the business meaning of the entities' connection. (See Appendix C for a list of meaningful verbs to use and avoid for entity relationships.)

4. **Identify and diagram the _cardinality_ and _optionality_ for each relationship.**

   - Determine the cardinality (i.e., the number of occurrences of one entity that are linked to a second entity) by showing the number of occurrences that can be linked for each set of relationships.

     - For each side of a given relationship, ask, "Can an occurrence of Entity A be related to one or more occurrences of Entity B?" Also ask, "Can an occurrence of Entity B be related to one or more occurrences of Entity A?"

     - Reconsider any one-to-one relationships, which are rare in most data models.

Cardinality Relationships

Cardinality Option	Meaning	Common Notation
1:1 (one to one)	A single occurrence of an entity is related to only one occurrence of the second entity, and a single occurrence of the second entity is related to only one occurence of the first entity.	
1: M (one to many)	A single occurrence of the first entity is related to one or more occurrences of the second entity, but a single occurrence of the second entity is related to only one occurrence of the first entity.	
M: M (many to many)	A single occurrence of the first entity is related to one or more occurrences of the second entity, and a single occurrence of the second entity is related to one or more occurrences of the first entity.	

- Determine the optionality (i.e., whether or not the relationship is mandatory).

  - Construct sentences to describe optionality, using the format "<Entity Name> ['must be' or 'may be'] <Relationship Name> ['one and only one' or 'one or more'] <Second Entity Name>."

  - Diagram the optionality using common notation (e.g., "A Contractor services zero or more Jobs" or "Each Job is to be serviced by one and only one Contractor").

Optionality Relationships

Optionality Option	Meaning	Common Notation
Mandatory One	A single occurrence of an entity is related to one and only one occurrence of the second entity.	
Optional One	A single occurrence of an entity is related to zero or one occurrence of the second entity.	
Mandatory One to many	A single occurrence of the first entity is related to one or many occurrences of the second entity.	
Optional Many	A single occurrence of the first entity is related to zero or many occurrences of the second entity.	

A data model with optionality and cardinality would show:

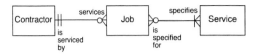

- Add the expected data volume by noting the minimum, maximum, and average number of instances above each entity.

- Diagram the entire model with cardinality and optionality to ensure that connections are maintained after the database is built and to prohibit "orphan data" (e.g., a Job with no servicing Contractor, or a Payment with no associated Job).

5. **Verify the data model.**

- Walk through available use case descriptions or scenarios, asking what data is needed. Be sure that all data is represented in the data model.

- Analyze the associations between entities and use cases with a CRUD matrix (i.e., entities are columns, use cases are rows, cells are populated with "create," "read," "update," or "delete.") This can reveal missing use cases or entities.

- Identify data attributes in the business rules and be sure each attribute is identified in the data model.

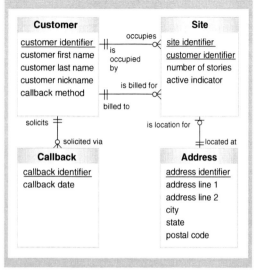

**Partial Data Model
for the CVGC Project**

Customer

<u>customer identifier</u>
customer first name
customer last name
customer nickname
callback method

Site

<u>site identifier</u>
<u>customer identifier</u>
number of stories
active indicator

occupies

is
occupied
by

is billed for

billed to

solicits

solicited via

is location for

located at

Callback

<u>callback identifier</u>
callback date

Address

<u>address identifier</u>
address line 1
address line 2
city
state
postal code

Tip

Involve data administrators or database administrators in the modeling process to elaborate and "normalize" the data model. (Normalizing eliminates data redundancy and reduces the risk that data will be corrupted once it is modified.) Have the database administrator use the normalized data model as a basis for designing the physical database.

∞∞∞ *Links to other models*

- Each entity should be defined in the glossary.
- Each data attribute (except possibly primary keys) can appear in use cases, scenarios, business rules, dialog maps, or prototypes.

Using business questions to derive the data model

A data model is an essential requirement model for analyzing requirements for any software that provides reporting, querying, or decision-support functionality. Supplement the data model with:

- Scenarios.
- Exploratory prototypes or *operational prototypes*.
- Business questions (i.e., example questions that business experts would ask of the completed system, or scenarios in the form of a query.) A template, like the one on the next page, can assist in eliciting and capturing business questions.

Business Questions for the CVGC Project

Business Question	Who Asks	Trigger	Business Justification	Decisions Made	Data Needed
What jobs do I need to complete today?	Contractor	Start of business day	Plan travel route; Gather equipment for loading the truck	Which materials to load onto truck and which order to use to resequence jobs	Postal Code, Address, Service, Customer Name, Customer Phone Number
Who can I schedule to complete a job estimate?	Scheduler	Customer requests on-site estimate	Turn estimates into scheduled jobs	Which contractors are available and who can be assigned to estimate	Contractor, Scheduled Completion Time by Day and Postal Code, Requesting Customer Address, Requesting Customer Postal Code

Variations

4.9.1 Class Model

A *class* is a generic definition for a collection of similar objects (i.e., person, places, events, and physical artifacts). Use a *class model* for projects employing object-oriented software development methods, tools, or databases.

An implementation-independent version of a class model is conceptually similar to a data model, although there will not be a direct correspondence between data entities in the data model and classes in the class model. A class model describes objects in the system and includes operations (behavior) in addition to data attributes. Other differences include variations in how relationships are described and the notation for cardinality and optionality. Projects employing object-oriented projects often create both a data model and a class model.

Partial Class Model
of the CVGC Project

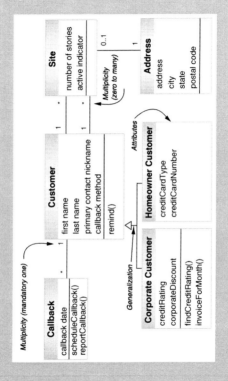

Site

number of stories
active indicator

0..1

Address

address
city
state
postal code

*Multiplicity
(zero to many)*

1

*

*

1

1

Attributes

Customer

first name
last name
primary contact nickname
callback method

remind()

Homeowner Customer

creditCardType
creditCardNumber

Generalization

Corporate Customer

creditRating
corporateDiscount

findCreditRating()
invoiceForMonth()

Multiplicity (mandatory one)

1

*

Callback

callback date

scheduleCallback()
reportCallback()

4.9.2 Data Dictionary

A data dictionary supplements the data model by providing a description of the data attributes and structures that the system needs. It is a central place to define each data element and describe its data type, length, and format. (Some project teams use data modeling tools that provide data dictionary capabilities.)

A common way to document the data dictionary is:

Symbol	Meaning
=	Description or list of attributes that comprise a data group
**	Freeform comment or definition
+	Attribute
min:max {}	Something repeated a minimum and maximum number of times
[| |]	Choices between several possibilities

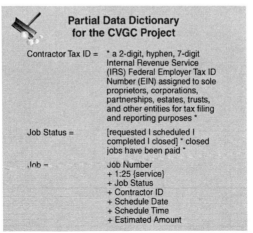

Partial Data Dictionary for the CVGC Project

Contractor Tax ID = * a 2-digit, hyphen, 7-digit Internal Revenue Service (IRS) Federal Employer Tax ID Number (EIN) assigned to sole proprietors, corporations, partnerships, estates, trusts, and other entities for tax filing and reporting purposes *

Job Status = [requested \| scheduled \| completed \| closed] * closed jobs have been paid *

Job = Job Number
+ 1:25 {service}
+ Job Status
+ Contractor ID
+ Schedule Date
+ Schedule Time
+ Estimated Amount

4.9.3 Sample *Data Tables*

Tables with sample data elicit and validate a data model or data dictionary. Each row represents a set of occurrences in an entity, and each column represents sample attributes.

CVGC Work Order Table

Work Order Number	Service	Customer ID	Schedule Date	Contractor Tax ID
3128	12 windows (exterior & interior)	378	May 16	76-1234567
5490	16 windows (exterior)	82	April 18	90-7654321
5490	Skylight	101	August 17	12-3456789

CVGC Contractor Table

Contractor Tax ID	First Name	Last Name	Social Security Number	Insurance Start Date	Work Area
12-3456789	Billie	Miller	xxx-xx-xxxx	Feb. 2005	54
84-7374943	Felicia	Graham	xxx-xx-xxxx	Aug. 2003	72
70-3210079	Hector	Davis	xxx-xx-xxxx	May 2002	18

4.10 State Diagram

What is it?

A state diagram is a visual representation of the life cycle of a data entity. Events trigger changes in data, resulting in a new state for that entity. Each state is a defined condition of an entity, a hardware component, or the entire system that requires data, rules, and actions. The state diagram can also show actions that occur in response to state changes.

Alternative names for this model

- State Machine Diagram
- State Transition Diagram

Why use it?

To understand how events impact data, and to identify missing requirements such as events, business rules, data attributes, use case preconditions, post-conditions, and steps.

What does it do?

- Identifies life cycle states of critical data entities
- Illustrates the sequence of states and the events that trigger state changes

Key questions that this model will answer

- What are the life cycle states of the key entities in the data model?
- What events trigger each life cycle change?
- What is the sequence of state changes?

How do I do it?

1. **Select the critical entities from the data model.**
   - Identify the entities with complex states.

- Look for nouns in the vision statement that are entities in the data model.

- Look for entities around which much of the user requirements revolve. Candidate entities frequently appear in use cases and business rules.

2. **For each selected entity, list possible life cycle states.**

   - Generate as many states as possible without evaluating or filtering the list. List specific, discrete states.

Life cycles include a beginning (how an occurrence of an entity is born, such as an "Opened" Job) and an ending (how an occurrence is terminated, such as an "Archived" Job).

Each state is an important condition or stage during the life cycle of an entity in which certain tasks are performed, rules are satisfied, or the entity waits for some event.

A state can be long-lived (days or weeks) or short-lived (milliseconds or hours).

3. **Reduce the list of states to those that apply to the product vision and the functionality within the product's scope.**

   - Review the meaning of each state, and combine those that are the same. For example, a Job in a "Proposed" state can mean the same as a Job in an "Estimated" state.

   - Eliminate states that are out of scope for the project. In our case study example, the states "Investigated," "Refunded," and "Reviewed" are not essential for meeting business goals and are not referred to in the other requirements models for the CVGC application.

4. **Arrange the states in time-ordered sequence.**

- Identify the starting (or initial) state and the final (or end) state.

- Define the order in which the states will happen and number them in sequence.

- Represent each state in a box (or rounded box, depending on which notation is used. Like data models, various styles and notation options are possible with state diagrams.)

5. **Identify triggering events for each transition.**

  - Reference the event-response table for business, temporal, and signal events that trigger state transitions.

 A transition is a change in state that is triggered by an event, such as a business or signal event originating from outside the system, a temporal event (e.g., a designated period of time), or a condition becoming true. An event can also trigger a transition to another state or back to the same state.

  - Draw lines connecting allowed state changes. Add arrowheads pointing into each allowable state in the sequence.

  - Label each transition line with the appropriate event.

  - Add newly discovered events to the event-response table.

  - Identify and draw discrete superstates with two or more substates (i.e., states within states. For example, a superstate of "Scheduled" Job might have substates of "Qualified," "Assigned," and "Notified.") Transitions can occur to and from substates as well as the superstate.

6. **Review related requirements for missing elements.**

  - Check that there are events identified to enter and exit each state or substate.

  - Evaluate any related user requirements for missing data, actions, or business rules.

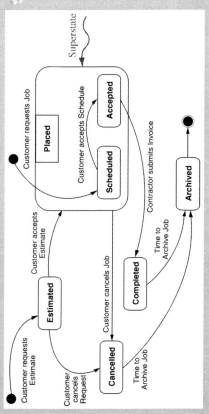

CVGC State Diagram

Superstate

Placed

Accepted

Scheduled

Customer accepts Schedule

Customer requests Job

Customer accepts Estimate

Estimated

Customer requests Estimate

Customer cancels Request

Cancelled

Customer cancels Job

Contractor submits Invoice

Completed

Time to Archive Job

Archived

Time to Archive Job

Tip Involve data modelers (as well as data administrators and database administrators) when modeling states because they have a solid understanding of the data. Create the data model (and class model, if used) concurrently with the state diagram.

 Links to other models

- Each state requires data in the data model to provide knowledge of that state.
- Each state transition will have one or more triggering events in the event-response table.
- State transitions are handled by one or more use cases.
- Business rules are associated with each state.

Variations

4.10.1 State-Data Matrix

A state-data matrix shows attributes that are added or changed during the state change. Be sure to identify each attribute in the data model and data dictionary.

CVGC State-Data Matrix for the Data Entity "Job"

State	Data Attributes			
Estimated	Estimation date	Estimation type (e.g., phone or on-site)	Estimated amount	Estimator name
Placed	Request date	Requesting customer	CVCG representative	
Placed (Substate: Scheduled)	Assign date	Assigned contractor		
Placed (Substate: Accepted)	Acceptance status			
Completed	Completion date	Actual amount	Callback date	
Cancelled	Cancel date	Cancel reason		
Archived	Archive date			

4.11 Business Rules

What are they?

Business rules are specific textual statements that decompose business policies. Business rules describe what defines, constrains, or enables the software behavior.

Why use them?

To specify the controls that govern user requirements and to clarify which rules should be enforced in software and which will be allocated to businesspeople. Because business rules require data, defining rules will uncover needed data. User requirements depend on the complete and correct enforcement of business rules.

What do they do?

- Represent decisions, calculations, and triggers for software
- Identify data to be compared, calculated, checked, and tested
- Enable businesspeople to rethink unnecessary or inefficient business rules

Key questions that this model will answer

- What must be true to support our policies?
- What checks must be made before actions are taken?
- What constrains actions and what must be true before an action can occur?
- What facts must be enforced in our data?
- What decisions are made?

Tip

Business rules focus on reasoning. For example, business rules for assigning contractors to jobs describe the necessary thinking for making job assignments. Business rules should be defined *independently* of who enforces them, and where, when, or how they are enforced.

Tip

Identifying and documenting business rules, regardless of how they will be implemented, enables businesspeople to rethink rules, remove unnecessary ones, or correct those that no longer serve business needs.

Categorizing Business Rules

Business rules fit into one of four categories: terms (including subcategories of derivations and inferences), facts, constraints, and action enablers.

Business Rules Categories

Category/ Subcategory	Meaning	Example
Terms	Nouns in the business and their definition. Terms constrain business concepts and are the building blocks for all other business rules. All business terms should be documented in the glossary.	"A Job is a set of services provided to a Customer at a specific location on a specific day."
Derivations	Calculations that use terms to arrive at new terms.	"Job Discount = (Job Total X Customer Discount)."
Inferences	Definitions of how knowledge is transformed by operating on terms and facts.	"A Customer who has paid for 2 or more Jobs in the prior 12 months is considered a Repeat Customer."
Facts	Necessary connections between terms. Facts can be documented as natural language sentences, as relationships on a data model, or as attributes of an entity in a data model.	"Each estimate must have an estimated-amount."
Constraints	Prohibits behavior or prevents information from being created or action from being taken if certain conditions are not met.	"Each Job must be scheduled within 7 working days of request."
Action Enablers	Conditions or facts that trigger actions.	"If a Job Completion Date is > 7 days after the Job Request Date, apply 5% discount to the total."

How do I do it?

1. **Identify the sources of business rules.**
   - Start with business policies and events from scope.
   - Refer to use cases, scenarios, the data model, and states, which provide the context for business rules.

2. **Ask questions to identify business rules.**
   - Focus on what needs to be known, calculated, decided, triggered, or constrained.
   - Document each business rule in natural language statements. Be sure each statement is declarative, with no sequencing implied.
   - Examine each business rule for inferences, derivations, or terms. Write any business rules that have not been documented.

Questions to Identify Business Rules

Source	Questions
All user requirements models and available documentation	What decisions are made? What must be true? What can go wrong and why is it wrong? What selections are made and how? When do exceptions occur? What approvals are needed? What validations must take place?
Use cases, scenarios, and events	What will prevent tasks from happening? What calculations are needed? What can and cannot happen?
Data model and states	What causes the state to change? What data must be present? What data might be wrong? Why? What must be known while in this state?

Tip Verbs such as "Validate," "Verify," "Match," "Decide," "Assess," "Determine," and "Evaluate" indicate that more detailed business rules need to be defined.

3. **Document the rules.**

- Determine whether each rule will be enforced in software or implemented by businesspeople as part of work procedures and business processes. (A work procedure such as "Scheduler signs an unpaid invoice after the Contractor provides a Job Completion Form" will not be enforced in software.)

- Identify useful attributes about business rules that will help validate the rules. (Examples include owner, jurisdiction, effective and expiry date, supporting business policy, version, category, type, and source.) Select only significant and useful attributes.

- Identify relationships between business rules and other user requirements. (For example, you can associate business rules with the use cases that require their enforcement.) A single business rule is often associated with multiple use cases. The business rule or a unique business rules-identifier assigned to each rule can be listed with each use case. Alternatively, you can create a matrix showing business rules, their attributes, and what use cases enforce those rules.

Tip Models that describe behavior, procedures, or tasks enforce business rules, and are not themselves business rules. Remove business rules from such models (e.g., use cases, scenarios, and process maps) and document them separately.

4. **Analyze the rules for consistency and necessity.**

- Check that no rule conflicts with another rule.

- Have businesspeople verify the correctness of business rules.

- Evaluate each rule for its necessity in supporting your business practice and policy. Remove unnecessary or out-of-date rules.

- Conduct walk-throughs of user requirement models (such as the event-response table and use cases) and ensure that each rule is enforced. Eliminate any unused rules.

 Identify all business rules, whether or not they will be implemented in software. Rethink each rule's utility and necessity. There is a cost for enforcing rules.

 Use business rules statements as the basis for error messages to end users in the operational system. This provides useful information and acts as a learning tool.

		CVGC Business Rules				
Business Rule Group	**Business Rule Identifier**	**Business Rule**	**Business Rule Category**	**Effective Date**	**Use Cases**	**Source**
Maintaining Customers	BR-2	If a Customer pays for more than one site, he is considered a Commercial Customer.	Inference	July 4	UC2 (Set Up Customer) UC4 (Provide Phone Estimate)	Jim Bean, Marketing Director
Invoicing	BR-18	If a Repeat Customer's Jobs exceed $5,000 in a continuous 12-month period, offer 15% discount.	Action enabler	July 4	UC4 (Provide Phone Estimate) UC13 (Pay for Job)	Pricing Guidelines, Version 5.6
Invoicing	BR-29	If a Customer is a Repeat Customer and a Corporate Customer, apply only the Corporate Customer Discount.	Constraint	September 17	UC4 (Provide Phone Estimate) UC13 (Pay for Job)	Pricing Guidelines, Version 5.6
Scheduling	BR-45	Overdue Payment Customers cannot schedule Jobs.	Constraint	August 12	UC5 (Schedule Job)	Scheduling Guidelines, Version 3.3

CCD Links to other models

- Terms, including derivations and inferences, should be defined in the glossary and appear as attributes or entities in a data model.

- Facts appear as attributes or as relationships between entities on a data model.

- Action enablers and constraints can be associated with use cases or states.

Variations

4.11.1 Atomic Business Rules

Each atomic business rule is a precise, formal statement that contains one discrete rule. The atomic business rules may break down a single business rules statement comprised of conditions and decisions that need to be tested to reach a conclusion or take some action.

Document atomic business rules with natural language templates that remove conditions that are mutually exclusive. Each template is formal grammar that follows precise conventions.

Many business rules are composite statements that you can decompose into multiple smaller business rules. Defining atomic business rules ensures that they are correctly implemented. For example, "If a customer is preferred or a customer is corporate, then offer 15% discount" is two distinct rules, one for each type of customer.

Format business rule templates as a left side, a connection, and a right side:

- The left side can contain conditions, events, and inferences.

- Multiple left sides can be combined with "and."

- The right side should not have multiple actions. Each action is a distinct atomic business rule.
- The action portion is supported by behavior represented in use case steps or in actions associated with state transitions.

Template Formats	Sample Atomic Business Rules
If <condition> then <action>	If repeat customer requests discount, then offer 5% discount for interior window cleaning line items.
On <event> then <action>	On customer anniversary then issue discount mailer
On <event> if <condition> then <action>	On close-of-week if outstanding payment then issue reminder letter
If <condition> then <conclusion>	If sum of service length for all services for a job is greater than 3 hours then consider job a half-day
<[qualified] term> <verb phrase> <non-verb phrase>	An overdue customer cannot request an estimate
<[qualified] term> must I must not <verb phrase> <non-verb phrase>	An overdue customer must not receive discounts

4.11.2 Decision Table

Decision tables specify complex business rules concisely in an easy-to-read tabular format. They document all of the possible conditions and actions that need to be accounted for in business rules. Conditions are factors, data attributes, or sets of attributes and are equivalent to the left side of atomic business rules. Actions are conclusions, decisions, or tasks and are equivalent to the right side of atomic business rules. Factors that must be evaluated form the top rows of the table. Actions make up the bottom rows of the table.

Software Requirements

Conditions								
Paid-to-date amount	$6501 or more	$4001-6500	$1000-4000	<$1000	$6501 or more	$4001-6500	$1000-4000	<$1000
Commercial Customer	N	N	N	N	Y	Y	Y	Y
Actions, Decisions, Conclusions								
Provide 5% discount	×	×	·	·	·	×	·	·
Provide 10% discount	·	·	·	·	×	·	·	·
Offer one free service	·	·	×	·	·	·	·	×
Offer two free services	·	·	·	·	·	·	×	·

4.11.3 Decision Trees

Decision trees are a graphical alternative to decision tables. A decision tree presents conditions and actions in sequence. Each condition is graphed with a decision symbol representing "yes" or "no" (or a "true" or "false" conclusion). Branches to additional conditions are drawn left-to-right. Actions are drawn inside rectangles to the right of the branch to which they apply.

CVGC Decision Tree

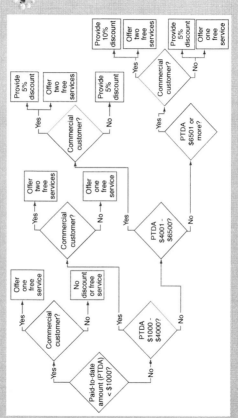

Tip Not all rules benefit from being depicted in a decision table or tree. Create decision tables or decision trees only for complex rules that have multiple factors or actions. Use either decision tables or decision trees, not both. Ask business experts which format ("table" or "tree") they prefer.

Good User Requirements Modeling Practices

Each requirements model describes one aspect of a problem. No single model can describe all requirements. Elements of one model link to elements of another, so each can be used to uncover related or missing elements in another model. For example, use cases thread to multiple models.

Models that Thread to and from Use Cases

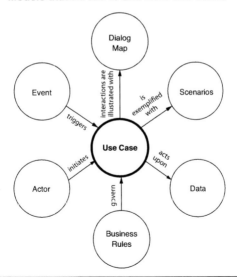

Different requirements models represent information at different levels of abstraction. A model such as a state diagram represents information at a high level of abstraction whereas detailed textual requirements represent a low level of abstraction. By stepping back from the "trees" (textual requirements) to look at the "forest" (a state diagram), you can discover requirements errors that are not evident when reviewing textual requirements alone.

Harvesting concepts from related requirements models

Because requirements models thread together, you can use various routes to develop one model from another. Select one model as a starting point and use its elements to develop another related model. For example, to understand user behavior when creating a dialog map, start with scenarios or a use case. To create a data model to describe the information requirements of the system, start with business questions or events.

Begin by creating and validating preliminary models at a high level early in requirements development. Identify ambiguous and questionable areas from those models, and iteratively elaborate on the details.

Create readable diagrams

Graphical user requirements models such as the context diagram, data model, and state diagram can become complex and difficult to read. Follow these practices to create diagrams with just enough information to be useful:

- Draw diagrams by hand to begin with, or with an easy-to-learn drawing tool.
- Allow for more space around the diagram so information is not crowded together or hard to read.

- Break larger models into multiple pages to increase readability.
- Organize the diagrams for readability, from left to right, and from top to bottom.
- Minimize lines crossing over symbols or other lines, which can be difficult to read and confusing to understand.
- Show only what is important, keeping the diagram simple. Selectively show details for areas that are particularly complex or controversial.
- Do not use all modeling elements just because they exist.
- Use naming conventions and glossary terms consistently across the diagrams.
- Focus on the accuracy and correctness of the diagram, not its beauty and comprehensiveness.

Adapted from Reference 9: Ambler, 2005

 Requirements models for mission- and life-*critical systems* are likely to require more detail to ensure they are correct and complete. Follow the guidelines above as you begin, allowing users to comfortably participate in reviewing the models. Extend these early models with additional details to fully define the user requirements.

4.12 Prioritized Requirements

What is it?

Requirements prioritization is the process of assigning a precedence that orders or ranks one requirement over another. Stakeholders need to understand the necessary trade-offs between requirements to allow them to make smart, defensible decisions about which requirements to implement and which to defer. Not all requirements are equally important or timely and there is rarely enough time and money to implement all requirements.

Alternative names for this technique

- Requirements Scrubbing
- Requirements Negotiation
- Requirements Triage

Why use it?

To allocate resources to the most important requirements and to make decisions about which requirements to implement and when to implement them. Prioritization can also help determine when to implement requirements in cases where product capabilities can be incrementally developed and deployed.

What does it do?

- Helps all stakeholders focus on the most essential requirements early in the process
- Surfaces trade-offs among competing project goals
- Minimizes politics and personal biases in the decision-making process
- Improves communications between customers and providers
- Creates more buy-in by stakeholders about what to design and build

---

- Helps control scope creep

- Provides a framework for ongoing prioritization when requirements evolve and change

- Helps plan software releases when requirements can be delivered incrementally

How do I do it?

1. **Identify and organize the requirements you need to prioritize.**

   - Make sure the requirements to be prioritized are at the same level of detail. Group related requirements. Use collections of use cases, use case packages, or use cases organized in a use case map to group requirements into features. (See section 5.2 for more on organizing requirements into features.)

   - Identify which features or requirements groups are subsumed by others. For example, "The System shall calculate the Job Total" is subsumed by the higher-level requirement "The System shall generate an Invoice." (See Chapter 5 for more on organizing and writing requirements.)

   - Identify requirements dependencies (which show when it is necessary to implement requirements together. For example, the set of requirements for "Invoicing" only make sense if the requirements for "Closing" are implemented.)

   - Identify which requirements may be interdependent and which can be implemented alone. For example, you can implement requirements for "Closing" without having to implement the "Invoicing" requirements, but not vice versa. (Requirements independence is sometimes possible where requirements can be fulfilled by manual processes already in place.)

   - Document requirements dependencies in a trace matrix (see section 7.3) or in a table format.

Requirements Dependencies Table

Feature Identification	Sub-Feature Name	Dependencies	Can Be Implemented Alone?
JM-1 (Job Management)	Estimating		Yes
JM-2	Scheduling	JM-1, CON-2	No
JM-3	Bidding		Yes
JM-4	Closing	JM-2	No
ACC-1 (Accounting)	Payment	JM-4	No
ACC-2	Invoicing	JM-4	No
CON-1 (Contractor Maintenance)	Geography Maintenance		Yes
CON-2	Contractor Maintenance		Yes
COM-1 (Company Maintenance)	Multi-Company Support		Yes
QRY-3 (Query)	Querying Scheduled Jobs	JM-2	Yes
RPT-1 (Reporting)	Callback Reporting	JM-4	Yes
RPT-8	Job History Reporting	JM-2, JM-4	Yes

Software Requirements

Tip Be sure to separate features from requirements. Also separate functional requirements from non-functional requirements.

2. **Assemble a team of stakeholders to participate in the prioritization process.**

   - For commercial software, include end users (if possible) and people from product development, sales, regulatory departments and agencies, and technical support. For systems developed for internal use, include end users and people from the regulatory department, the product champions' business departments (including product development, sales, or marketing), and technical support.

   - Include technical staff (such as designers, developers, and the project manager) as advisors to the prioritization process. The technical staff should be familiar with any existing software and with the risks associated with the project.

   - Keep the prioritization team small (i.e., fewer than seven people). In large projects, you may need to increase this number so make sure the prioritization process is well facilitated, that all stakeholders are familiar with the requirements you are prioritizing, and use decision rules and a decision-making process.

3. **Identify the criteria to consider.**

   - Rank each requirement according to how well it meets each criterion. Criteria are factors that help assess the relative importance of the requirements based on how well the requirement will achieve that criterion.

Tip Prioritization criteria vary by project. Example criteria include customer value, cost, difficulty, time to market, technical risk, economic value, regulatory compliance, product stability, ease of deployment, provision of a competitive advantage, contractual commitments, technical reuse, and resistance to change. Select a subset of criteria that is critical to making a sound decision.

4. **Determine the relative importance of the criteria.**

   • Compare the criteria in pairs. Ask, "Is <Criteria A> more important than <Criteria B>?"

   • Assign a higher weight to criteria that are more important than others. (For example, you would weight "Time to Market" or "Minimal Organizational Change" higher than other criteria, if these criteria are deemed to be of greater importance.) If all criteria are equally important, no weighting is needed.

5. **Create a criteria matrix to show the strength of the correlation between the requirement and the criteria.**

   • Place the features (i.e., sets of use cases, logically related requirements statements, or whatever groupings of logically related requirements you defined in the first step) in the rows of the matrix. Each row should include one or more features that can be released independently. (For example, requirements for the features "Scheduling" and "Estimating" will be implemented together, but the feature "Querying Scheduled Jobs," while dependent on the Scheduling feature, can be implemented alone.)

   • Use a 3, 6, 9 scale (or other ranking mechanism) to separate the value of the rankings. Score requirements with a low correlation to the criteria as a 3, those with a medium correlation as a 6, and those with a strong correlation as a 9.

- Have participants evaluate each feature against the criteria and discuss their ranking. Ask participants to explain the rationale for their rankings and arrive at a group ranking. If there are more than seven participants, consider asking them to do their rankings individually, collate them, then discuss and review the findings before arriving at a group ranking.

- Calculate the importance of each feature by totaling the ranking of each criterion. If any criteria are weighted, calculate the weighted score by multiplying the feature's score for that criterion by the weight given.

- Repeat this process for each feature.

- Have stakeholders review the results and discuss them, explaining their scorings. (This is an opportunity to learn about different perspectives. For example, technical staff may not know market or customer needs while business staff may not know about technical risks.)

 Tip   Use symbols when displaying the matrix to stakeholders to allow visual cues to aid in discussing the matrix. Use a double circle for strong correlation (9), a single circle for moderate correlation (6), a triangle for weak correlation (3), and no symbol when no correlation exists between the criteria and the requirement.

◎	○	△	
Strong	Moderate	Weak	None

| Weight | **9** | **6** | **3** | **0** |

CVGC Weighted Criteria Matrix

Criteria Dependent Features	Streamline Operations (Weighting: 2)	Customer Value	Technical Risk	Total Score
Estimating + Scheduling	◉	◉	○	33
Bidding	△	○	◉	21
Closing + Invoicing	◉	○	○	30
Payment	◉	△	◉	30
Geography Maintenance	△	○	△	15
Contractor Maintenance	◉	◉	△	30
Multi-Company Support	△	○	◉	21
Querying Scheduled Jobs	○	◉	○	27
Callback Reporting	◉	○	○	30
Job History Reporting	○	△	△	18

 Tip Use the criteria matrix for requirements that are negotiable, not for those that implement nonnegotiable requirements or provide essential competitive or organizational capabilities.

6. Decide which requirements to deliver.

- Use the matrix to focus discussion on what requirements to deliver and when to deliver them. Be sure to consider project constraints (e.g., resources and time).

- Discuss trade-offs among requirements (e.g., providing customer value vs. managing technical risk). Surface issues (e.g., team culture, technical skills, familiarity with the business domain, and availability of subject matter experts) that impact the team's probability of success.

- Consider options such as incremental software delivery. Generate release strategies (i.e., combinations of requirements to implement over time). Consider the development time to implement, feature dependencies, probability of success, and business value when arriving at a release strategy.

CVGC Release Schedule

Release Number	Features to be Implemented
1	Contractor Maintenance, Estimating, Scheduling
2	Querying Scheduled Jobs, Closing, Payment, Invoicing
3	Job History Reporting, Callback Reporting
4	Geography Maintenance, Bidding
5	Multi-Company Support

Use the matrix as a tool to make decisions, not as the decision itself. Be sure the decision-making process is clearly identified and followed before making the decision. State the circumstances under which you will review and modify the requirements decision.

Variations

4.12.1 Prioritize Requirements Based on Value, Cost, and Risk

Use a standard set of criteria, such as value, cost, and risk, to construct a prioritization matrix:

- *Value* is composed of (a) the benefit to the customer or business if the requirements are implemented, and (b) the penalty to the customer or business if the requirements are not implemented. Value consists of the market or organizational utility of features (benefit) and the downside of lost revenue, dissatisfied customers, or regulatory violations (penalty).

- *Cost* is the expense of implementing the feature, taking into consideration the effort, resources, and capital costs.

- *Risks* are the technical risks associated with implementing the requirement. Risks are any occurrences that can prevent or seriously hamper the team's ability to deliver the requested functionality. Risks include factors such as the degree of technical complexity, use of new technologies, inexperienced staff, or dependence on external software components.

Be sure to have the appropriate stakeholders rank the requirements. For example, have sponsors or marketing staff rank for value and have technical staff rank for cost and technical risk. Assign numeric values on a scale of 1 to 9. The higher the number, the more strongly the requirements meet the criteria. For example, a relative benefit of 9 means that that feature will be extremely valuable for users, whereas a benefit of 1 means that it will not be very useful. Calculate the sum of the four ratings (benefit, penalty, cost, and risk) for all of the features or functional requirements being prioritized.

Software Requirements

Calculate the percentage of the total value contributed by each of the requirements being prioritized by dividing the number of value "points" for that requirement by the grand total for all requirements. Similarly, calculate the percentage of the total cost that comes from each requirement and the percentage of the total technical risk from each requirement.

Calculate priority as:

$$\frac{\text{Value \% (Sum of Benefit and Penalty)}}{\text{(Cost \%) + (Risk \%)}}$$

Sort the requirements or features in descending order when you have finished calculating priority. The features with the highest calculated priority numbers have the best balance of value, cost, and risk, and should have the highest priority.

As with the weighted criteria matrix, use this matrix to prioritize those requirements that are negotiable, not ones that are mandatory. Use this prioritization scheme as a guideline, not a decision.

See Reference 8: Wiegers, 2003 for more details on this technique.

CVGC Requirements Prioritization Based on Value, Cost, and Risk

Criteria / Features	Benefit	Penalty	Total Value	Percent Value	Cost	Percent Cost	Risk	Percent Risk	Priority
Job History Reporting	5	4	9	8	2	3.9	1	2.1	1.3
Contractor Maintenance	7	6	13	11.5	3	5.9	2	4.3	1.13
Querying Scheduled Jobs	8	7	15	13.3	4	7.8	2	4.3	1.11
Callback Reporting	6	5	11	9.7	3	5.9	3	6.4	0.79
Geography Maintenance	4	2	6	5.3	3	5.9	1	2.1	0.66
Closing + Invoicing	7	8	15	13.3	7	13.7	6	12.8	0.50
Estimating + Scheduling	8	9	17	15	8	15.7	7	14.9	0.49
Payment	6	7	13	11.5	5	9.8	8	17	0.43
Multi-Company Support	7	2	9	8	8	15.7	9	19.1	0.23
Bidding	2	3	5	4.4	8	15.7	8	17	0.13
Totals	60	53	113	100	51	100	47	100	

Information adapted from Reference 8: Wiegers, 2003

Software Requirements

4.12.2 Simple Prioritization

For small projects with few requirements, use a simple prioritization process. Choose a ranking scheme, assemble a team of stakeholders to participate in the prioritization, and rank the requirements. Use a ranking scheme such the MoSCoW scheme (see section 3.5 for more information on the MoSCoW scheme) and modify the meanings for your specific project.

Modified MoSCoW Scheme

Ranking	Meaning
Must	Inclusion of the requirement is mandatory. The software product is not acceptable or is unusable without it.
Should	The requirement is important but not mandatory. Without the requirement, there will be significant loss of user utility or market share. Although this requirement would enhance the software product, the software product is still acceptable in its absence.
Could	Customers and users can live without this feature if it is going to cost too much or cause a delay in delivery of "Must" requirements. Delivery of these requirements can be postponed.
Won't	This requirement will not be considered for inclusion in the software product at all or at this time.

Tip Use a forced distribution to ensure that stakeholders compare the relative importance of the set of requirements. Tell them they cannot assign more than 25% of the requirements to each ranking (i.e., assign no more than 25% to "Must," no more than 25% to "Should," etc.).

4.12.3 Quality Function Deployment Matrix

Quality function deployment (QFD) is a methodology for analyzing customer needs, priorities, and benchmark information. It requires compiling information and organizing it into seven areas on a matrix. See GOAL/QPC's *The Design for Six Sigma Memory Jogger*™ for more information on constructing a QFD Matrix.

CHAPTER
5

Specify
the Requirements

Requirements specification is the process of elaborating, refining, and organizing requirements into documentation. The specification of requirements is primarily the responsibility of the analyst, but should involve the users who verify the requirements documentation and the providers who use the requirements documentation to produce the software product.

How do I specify requirements?

To specify requirements:

1. **Document the user requirements.**

   • Document the requirements from the user's point of view in a user requirements document (described later in this chapter). Include analysis models and narrative prose.

Tip   Some organizations may choose not to create a separate user requirements document but will instead incorporate requirements into the software requirements specification. Other organizations, especially those developing complex systems, benefit from having a separate document that describes how the software will operate and impact the user's environment (referred to as the "operational environment"). The requirements that you document during specification can take the form of either of these two documents (the software requirements specification or user requirements document) or be one combined document.

- Describe the characteristics and behavior of the proposed system from the user's point of view. (This description will act as a bridge between user needs and the software requirements specification.)

2. Verify the user needs.

- Check that the user requirements describe what users need to do with the system.

- Ensure the requirements are derived from business requirements (i.e., the product vision and stated project goals and objectives).

- Have stakeholders check that the requirements are complete, consistent, and of high quality. Revise the documentation as needed.

3. Document the software requirements.

- Record the software requirements in a software requirements specification.

- Write the specification document for the provider audience (who provide the software). Describe the functional requirements, quality attributes, system interfaces, and design and implementation constraints.

4. Verify the software requirements.

- Be sure that the documentation correctly describes the intended capabilities and characteristics of the system.

- Check that software requirements have been accurately derived from user requirements, system requirements, and other sources.

- Be sure the documentation and requirements specification provide an adequate basis to proceed with design, construction, and testing.

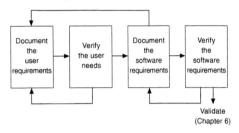

| Document the user requirements | Verify the user needs | Document the software requirements | Verify the software requirements |

Validate
(Chapter 6)

Tip

Be sure documentation conforms to your organization's templates, standards, and naming conventions. Establish procedures for documentation change control to monitor any changes to documents.

Beware!

Writing a user requirements document or software requirements specification is not a substitute for direct, person-to-person interaction with knowledgeable users. As much as possible, involve actual subject matter experts. For commercial software efforts, substitute surrogate or proxy users for real users who may be unavailable.

What Tools and Techniques Will I Use to Specify Requirements?

When you need to:	Then create:
Document and verify user requirements	A User Requirements Document
Document and verify software requirements	A Software Requirements Specification

5.1 User Requirements Document

What is it?

A user requirements document is a record of requirements written for a user audience that describes what users need and why they need it.

Alternative names for this document

- Use Case Document
- Concept of Operations (ConOps)
- Requirements Definition
- System Definition

Why use it?

To obtain agreement on what the product must do to satisfy user requirements, to consolidate the needs of diverse user communities, and to provide additional detail not described by analysis models. The user requirements document also acts as a bridge between defining business and software requirements.

What does it do?

- Formalizes requirements elicited from all users and customers

- Presents requirements at a high level

- Provides background information, target environment, functional needs, and quality attributes

- Provides a basis for deriving software requirements specification details

Key questions that this document will answer

- What do users need to do with the system?

- What are some examples of how the system will operate?

- What might change for users once the system is implemented?

How do I do it?

1. **Identify sources for the user requirements document.**

   - Include the product vision, project charter, analysis models, user procedural documentation (e.g., manuals, standard operating procedures, and training materials), any current system documentation, and any other documentation about user needs.

   - Decide on the format for the requirements documentation. (A suggested format is provided on the next page, or you can use your organization's standard document templates if they are available.) Use richer documentation when outsourcing development to an external provider, or if the product is a complex or critical system.

User Requirements Outline

1. Introduction
   1.1 Purpose and background
   1.2 Overview of business and user needs
   1.3 Document overview and conventions
   1.4 References
2. Current system or situation
   2.1 Background, objectives, and scope of the current system or situation
   2.2 Current system or business processes
   2.3 People, organizations, and locations
3. Justification for the new system
   3.1 Rationale for the new system
   3.2 Overview of the system and impacted business processes
   3.3 Affected people, roles, and organizations
   3.4 Priorities and scope of the change
   3.5 Impact on operations, the organization, people, and support
   3.6 Impact on policies, regulations, and business rules
4. New functionality
   4.1 User and user profiles
   4.2 New or changed user capabilities (also see Appendix D)
   4.3 Impact of the new capabilities on existing user processes and systems
   4.4 Interfaces with other systems
   4.5 User support environment and user documentation
5. Evaluation of the proposed system
   5.1 Advantages, disadvantages, and limitations
   5.2 Business and organization change management plan
   5.3 Operational issues
   5.4 Alternatives considered

Appendices
A: Glossary of terms
B: Data dictionary
C: Context diagram
D: Use cases and scenarios

---

2. **Organize the user requirements into the user requirements document.**

- Use analysis models (e.g., use cases for the "New processes" section, a context diagram to illustrate "Interfaces with other systems," and business rules in the "Impact on policies, regulations, and business rules" section) to structure the document.

- Review the document from the perspective of various business readers (i.e., the project sponsor, business managers, marketing or product managers, trainers, and users).

- Check that the document uses the user's terminology, with technical jargon removed.

- Be sure the language in the document is clear.

 Supplement user requirements with a draft of the user manual, an operational prototype, or both.

 Projects involving large, complex systems may supplement or substitute a user requirements document (or Concept of Operation [ref: IEEE STD 1362-1998]. See Appendix A for additional IEEE references) with a system requirements specification [ref: IEEE STD 1233] that describes system interactions, external interfaces, and other performance capabilities.

5.2 Software Requirements Specification Document

What is it?

The software requirements specification (SRS) document is a precise record of requirements that enables software providers to design, develop, and test the software solution. The SRS document [ref: IEEE STD 830-1998] contains the entire set of prioritized functional and nonfunctional requirements that the software product must satisfy.

(The SRS may be supplemented by user requirements documentation, including analysis models).

Alternative names for this document

- Specification
- Requirements Document
- Functional Specification
- Technical Specification

Why use it?

To document the functional requirements, quality attributes, constraints, and external interfaces for the software solution. The SRS also serves as a contract between customers and the provider organization.

What does it do?

- Transforms analysis models, user requirements information, and system requirements (for complex systems) into precise textual statements
- Incorporates analysis models directly into the software requirements specification
- Supplies the details necessary to design and code the software product
- Provides the basis for creating test plans and procedures
- Serves as a source for creating user documentation (e.g., user manuals, training materials, tutorials, and job aids)
- Identifies mandatory requirements and the relative importance of the requirements

---

Key questions that this document will answer

- What behaviors and capabilities must the software provide?

- What constraints on the software solution must be adhered to?

- What qualities or characteristics are needed for the software?

How do I do it?

1. **Identify and label the features needed to achieve the software goals.**

   - Review requirements information (including the product vision statement, analysis models, user requirements documentation, and information from requirements elicitation activities) to identify features. Each feature is a set of cohesive capabilities needed to achieve business or mission goals (e.g., "manage contractors," "balance books," or "detect signal").

   - Name the features as a short description (e.g., "schedule jobs") or in a "gerund" format (e.g., "scheduling"). Uniquely label each feature by including numbers (e.g., 1.0, 2.0, 3.0), letters (e.g., FEA-1, FEA-2, FEA-3, for "feature"), or abbreviations (e.g., SCH.JOB and MAI.CON, for the features "schedule jobs" and "maintain contractors") that will enable you to decompose the textual requirements further. (Labels are important to distinguish requirements from one another while also documenting how the requirements are de-composed.)

   - Use the feature name in the SRS as a label for the functional requirements within each feature. Write a brief description and state the relative priority for each feature. (Use an agreed-upon prioritization

---

scheme to prioritize the features. Chapter 4 provides information to help you prioritize requirements.)

Features are not the only way to organize functional requirements. Other approaches include:

- Scan the vision statement for verbs that summarize software capabilities.

- Group a single use case, groups of logically related use cases, or use case packages (depending on their granularity).

- Find names of related user goals or tasks.

- Organize sets of event-response pairs.

- Define the functionality that manages groupings of similar data inputs and outputs.

- Pair together pre- and post-conditions from use cases or events.

2. **Decompose and document the functional requirements within each feature.**

• Break down the features into functional requirements. Visualize the end result as a hierarchy.

CVGC Functional Hierarchy

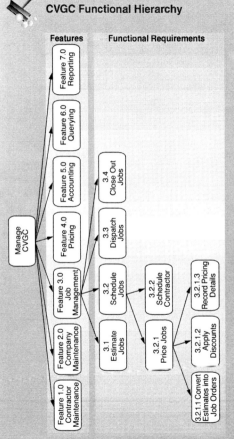

Features **Functional Requirements**

Manage CVGC

Feature 1.0 Contractor Maintenance
Feature 2.0 Company Maintenance
Feature 3.0 Job Management
Feature 4.0 Pricing
Feature 5.0 Accounting
Feature 6.0 Querying
Feature 7.0 Reporting

3.1 Estimate Jobs
3.2 Schedule Jobs
3.3 Dispatch Jobs
3.4 Close Out Jobs

3.2.1 Price Jobs
3.2.2 Schedule Contractor

3.2.1.1 Convert Estimates into Job Orders
3.2.1.2 Apply Discounts
3.2.1.3 Record Pricing Details

- Write short, concise sentences using imperatives to describe the functional requirements (e.g., "The system shall prompt the scheduler for the job date"). Use a standard sentence structure such as:

[<restriction>] <subject> <action verb> [<observable result>] [<qualifier>]

where:

- **[<restriction>]** identifies the conditions under which the requirement must be satisfied.

- **<subject>** shows who or what is doing the task (generally "the system" or an actor).

- **<action verb>** is the task being performed.

- **[<observable result>]** shows the outcome of the action.

- **[<qualifier>]** identifies the quality attributes for the requirement.

    Note: The brackets "[ ]" indicate optional components of the sentence.

Examples Describing Functional Requirements

Example with no restriction: "The system shall allow a scheduler to select services to be included in the job."

Example with restriction: "When no contractor is available in the customer's postal code, the system shall allow the scheduler to select from a list of nearby postal codes."

Example with restriction, observable result, and qualifier: "When a contractor approves a job, the system shall generate a dispatch ticket to the contractor within thirty seconds after the approval data is stored in the system."

- Use the active voice so that the subject is the performer of the action that is denoted by the verb (e.g., "When the scheduler assigns a contractor to a job, the system shall lock the time slot for that contractor" is active; "When a contractor is scheduled for a job, the time slot is locked" is passive).

- Use continuances (i.e., phrases that follow an imperative and introduce a lower level requirement) to decompose requirements statements (e.g., "The system shall provide a list of available contractors in the following order:..."). Continuances include "below:", "as follows:", "following:", "listed:", and "in particular:".

- Provide examples immediately following what is to be illustrated. State "for example..." or "this is an example."

- Break complex or compound requirement statements into multiple statements. (Complex statements describe sequence and flow (doing something after something else). Compound statements use conjunctions (e.g., "and," "or," "also," "with").)

- Break down nested conditional clauses into separate statements. For example, the nested conditional clause: "If the scheduler requests a specific contractor who is unavailable on the request date, then the system shall display the next available dates and time slots for that contractor, else if the scheduler requests an alternative date, then the system shall display available dates and time slots for any available contractor" should be broken down into "When a scheduler requests a specific contractor who is unavailable on the request date, the system shall display the contractor's next three available dates and time slots" and "When the scheduler requests an alternative date, the system shall display dates and time slots for up to seven available contractors."

- Look for exceptions (such as "not," "if," "but," "unless," "although," and "except") and break them into distinct requirements statements. (Requirements with exceptions may reflect a business rule and result in additional business rules.)

- Reference business rules after requirements statements (e.g., "The system shall provide the scheduler with a list of available contractors to assign to the job [ref: BR-5, BR-12, and BR-23].") or supplement the SRS with a *requirements trace matrix* (described in section 7.3) that associates requirements and business rules.

- Cite the business rules document as an external reference or reference them in the appendix.

- Use tables or charts to explain complex requirements. Title each table or chart with a unique identifier for easy identification. Identify the purpose of the table or chart in the text immediately preceding it. Cite references clearly and correctly with a unique identifier (e.g., "See Job States, Appendix B, Figure 5") and fully cite any external documents with the document name, location, and unique identifier.

- Uniquely label each lower level requirement so that its hierarchical association to its higher level requirements is clear (e.g., "3.1.1, 3.1.2, 3.1.3," "SCH.JOB-1.0, SCH.JOB-1.1, SCH.JOB-1.2.1," or "SCH.JOB.TotalCost" (to abbreviate functional requirements providing the total cost in the "schedule job" feature)).

 Tip A single use case can translate into multiple functional requirements statements within a feature. Each use case step is a candidate lower level functional requirement within each function.

**Multiple Functional
Requirements Statements
within a Feature**

1.0 Scheduling   *Feature name*

  1.1 Schedule job   *Use case name*

    1.1.1 The system   *Use case step*
       shall allow the
       scheduler to select
       an estimated job.

3. **Verify the functional requirements statements.**

   • Be sure to define each business term used in textual
     requirements in the glossary. Include the glossary in
     the appendix of the SRS, or cite the glossary as an
     external document to reference.

   • Make sure that you can verify each requirement
     statement (i.e., test it in some way). Be sure to
     clearly and distinctly write algorithms, decisions,
     and conditions ("If...then...") and document each
     in only one location in the SRS.

   • Involve testers in reviewing or developing re-
     quirements to ensure that the requirements can be
     tested.

   • Be sure that you define all of the data needed to
     satisfy functional requirements in the data model
     (or class model or data dictionary). Include the data
     model in either the analysis model appendix or the
     functional requirements section of the SRS.

   • Remove or clarify any requirements noted as "to be
     determined" (TBD).

Tip

Construct questions about each requirements statement to verify that it is unambiguous. If any question cannot be answered, break the statement down into additional requirements statements as needed or add information to other portions of the requirements information (i.e., the glossary, data dictionary, or business rules).

Example Questions to Check for Ambiguity

Requirement statement: The system shall invoice customers for jobs at month-end.

Questions: What is an invoice? What information does it contain? Will the invoice amount ever be adjusted for any reason? Do all customers get an invoice? When is month-end? Do all jobs get invoiced or only certain ones? In what format is the invoice provided (e.g., print, electronic, or fax)?

Answering these questions can result in additional documentation such as a glossary definition for an invoice, a statement naming the attributes of an invoice (or a data dictionary entry for an invoice), a business rule for when invoices are adjusted, a restriction statement for the original functional requirement statement, or conditions for printing the invoice.

4. **Identify and quantify the quality attributes.**

- Describe the quality attributes as characteristics of the software's operation, development, and deployment.

Software Requirements

Quality Attributes

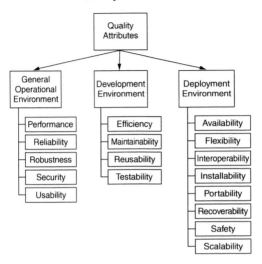

- Review the list of quality attributes and select those that are applicable.

- Specify metrics for all of the quality attributes. Provide a scale of measurement (i.e., the units that you will use to test conformance of the product) along with timescales, acceptance values, minimum and maximum values, or any other metrics needed to test conformance. Add them as qualifiers to functional requirements statements if they have not been added already.

Example Attribute
with Metrics

QA-1: Estimators shall be able to view details for a quote within seven seconds of pressing the Enter key after entering customer details.

- Remove jargon, abbreviations, or acronyms (e.g., "point and click," "plug and play," "high fidelity," "WYSIWYG," and "UI").
- Create derived requirements by breaking down higher level quality attributes into multiple discrete quantifiable statements.

Derived Requirements

Higher level attribute:
QA-2: The system shall be available for use by office staff from 7 a.m. PST to 7 p.m. PST, Monday through Friday.

Derived requirements:
QA-2.1: All batch processing (i.e., file loads and standard reports) shall be executed and completed between 8 p.m. and 5 a.m. PST.
QA-2.2: All system administration functions (i.e., backup and maintenance) shall be performed on Sunday.

- Uniquely label each quality requirement using numbers (e.g., "6.1, 6.1.2, 6.2" for the section in which quality attributes reside in the SRS), letters, or abbreviations (e.g., SEC-1.3, PER-3, USE-4, for "security," "performance," and "usability").

Tip

Possible quality attributes, their meanings, and suggested metrics are provided in Appendix E. Ambiguous words and phrases to avoid when describing quality attributes are provided in Appendix F.

 Tip

Quality attributes are essential to critical systems so be sure to include quality attributes for reliability, availability, maintainability, safety, and security in these systems.

 Beware!

Failing to document specific quality attributes is risky. It is more expensive and risky to introduce these requirements later in development, although quality attributes may truly be unknown when new technology is being deployed or when the software will implement a new application of existing technology.

5. **Quantify the functional requirements.**

- Assign measures or explicit criteria to the functional requirements. Relate the quantification to the accuracy of the results, look and feel (usability), security, maintainability, portability, or performance of the functionality. Consider speed of response (e.g., response time in seconds), throughput (e.g., number of transactions per period of time), capacity (e.g., number of concurrent users), and execution timing for software involving hardware (e.g., completing a robotic arm operation within 100 milliseconds) in your performance quantification.

 Quantified Functional Requirements

SCH.JOB-1.3: The estimated job total shall be "plus or minus" 10% of the actual invoice.
SCH.JOB-2.4: The system shall be capable of storing a maximum of 10,000 active estimates.

6. **Associate related requirements.**

    - Provide functional requirements with references to related quality attributes. (A quality attribute may be required by multiple functional requirements. For example, certain response times and reliability requirements may be required by several functional requirements.)

Associated Requirements

SCH.JOB-1.1: The system shall provide the scheduler with a list of available contractors for the requested job's postal code. [RES-3]

You can also show related requirements in a matrix.

Partial Functional and Quality Attributes Trace Matrix

Quality Attribute	Functional Requirements		
	SCH.JOB-1.0	SCH.JOB-2.0	MAI.COM-1.0
PER-1.1	X	X	
PER-2.1	X		
SEC-1.1		X	
SEC-2.1			X
THR-1.1		X	

7. Identify the design and implementation constraints.

 Tip Design constraints limit how you can design the software. Implementation constraints restrict the environment that the software will operate within. Both types of constraints are imposed on the product, usually by management policy. (Designers and architects should identify or review constraints.)

- Consider:
  - Design and development languages, tools, data interchange formats, and programming and design conventions and standards.
  - Regulations and policies.
  - Restrictions imposed by required hardware interfaces such as limits on memory utilization, processor limits, size, or weight.

Design and Implementation Constraints

DC-1: The system shall use Daedalus SQL Server 6005.

DC-2: The system shall operate with the following Web browsers: Saturn Browser 6.0 or below, and Shetland 7.1 and above.

DC-3: The system shall conform to Sumplus GUI standards.

- Specify versions, vendor, and any other identifying information. Provide the rationale for the constraint. Cite any necessary compliance with corporate hardware and software standards and technologies.

Specified Constraints

The system shall operate on BigKnat Operating System Versions 4.5 and higher. Reference CorpStd-SysSoft-487, 2004.

8. Identify the external interface requirements.

Tip External interfaces are shared boundaries between the product and other systems or subsystems. Interfaces are to users, hardware, and software.

- Document each interfacing component and define the format of each interface. Specify each interface with the name, version or release number, vendor, and any other identifying information.

CVGC Interfacing Components

EI-1: The system shall interface with Quad4-Tech Laser Printers for printing invoices and checks.

- Consider:
  - Characteristics of the appearance of all user interfaces (including screen layout and navigation standards, use of function keys or buttons, help, shortcuts, message standards and layout, report layouts, and any input or output interfaces to users).
  - Hardware components (including the type of device and the configuration characteristics of the device).

- Software components such as:
  - Operating systems and browsers that communicate with Web servers that provide services over the Internet.
  - Communications software that represents and transfers data among computer systems or networks (e.g., messaging software, communication protocols, e-mail, and encryption software).
  - Networking software that monitors and controls information exchange in a networking environment.
  - Directory software that maintains knowledge of the location of network resources.
  - Commercial components and interfaces to other software application systems.

9. **Remove any design solutions.**
  - Remove any constraints on how the product must be implemented unless they are legitimate design constraints for the developing or implementing organization. Allow designers to find the best alternatives, given the requirements and known design constraints.

 Removing Design Constraints

With design constraints: "The system shall prompt for user name and passwords when accounting functions are requested."

After removing design constraints: "The system shall ensure that only authorized users can access accounting functions."

---

10. Identify and correct missing, conflicting, and overlapping requirements.

 Tip Missing requirements leave gaps that create design and development errors. Conflicting requirements have opposing meanings, negate each other, or negatively impact each other. Overlapping requirements have elements of one requirement stated in another.

- Use scenarios to uncover missing requirements. Conduct scenario walk-throughs of the requirements document to detect errors.

- Associate use cases with requirements statements, if use cases are available. Store the information in a requirements trace matrix as an aid for detecting any overlaps or missing requirements.

Use Cases Traced to Functional Requirements

Functional Requirement	Use Case		
	UC5	UC8	UC11
SCH.JOB-1.0	↵		
SCH.JOB-2.0			↵
MAI.COM-1.0		↵	
MAI.COM-2.1		↵	
MAI.CON-1.0			
MAI.CON-1.1	↵		

- Review functional requirements for missing quantification or associated quality attributes.

- Review events from the event-response table. Ask if all of the data, actions, and business rules are specified to process each event. Be sure there are quality attributes (such as capacity and response time) for handling each event.

• Create CRUD matrices for each entity or attribute in the data model. Look for empty cells, indicating that a requirement is missing or the data attribute is unnecessary.

CRUD Matrix for the Entity "Job Order"

Data Attributes	Functional Requirement			
	SCH.JOB-1.0	SCH.JOB-2.0	MAI.COM-1.0	MAI.COM-2.1
Contractor Tax ID	C	U	R	U, D
Contractor Active Indicator	C	R, U	U	D
Contractor Payment Method	C,R	R	U	
Contractor Service				

Missing Functional Requirement

- Create a matrix to detect overlapping and conflicting requirements. (Empty cells indicate no overlaps or conflicts.) Remove overlaps from requirements statements by writing shorter, independent statements. Research conflicting requirements by referencing requirements sources and consulting with stakeholders.

Overlapping and Conflicting Requirements

Requirement ID \ Requirement ID	FR-1.1	FR-1.2	QR-1.1	QR-1.2
FR-1.1		Overlapping		
FR-1.2	Overlapping			Conflict
QR-1.1				
QR-1.2		Conflict		

 Tip Certain quality attributes can conflict with other quality attributes. (For example, response time can conflict with capacity, and security can conflict with usability or response time.) Find any conflicts and address them with stakeholders. Negotiate requirements trade-offs before design begins.

11. **Prioritize all requirements, add requirements attributes, and trace the priorities and attributes to each requirement.**

- Review the priorities from your analysis of requirements (see Chapter 4 for more information on requirements priorities) and revise them as needed. Assign a priority to requirements at an appropriate level of detail (such as features or groups of functional requirements).

Beware!

Lowest level requirements statements (also called leaf requirements statements) are often too granular for assigning priorities.

- Identify other attributes that are important to define about requirements. Cross-reference attributes to requirements in requirements trace matrices. (See section 7.2 for more information on requirements attributes).

12. **Organize the requirements into a SRS template and complete each section.**

- Write a high-level overview of the software product and include a description of its purpose, scope, context, and business goals. (Refer to the vision statement, if necessary). If the product is part of a larger system, illustrate and describe how it relates to the larger system.

- Describe stakeholders and users, or reference the user requirements document.

- Describe what user documentation will be provided with the product. (This can include manuals, training materials, job aids, tutorials, and help facilities within the software product.)

- Describe any assumptions (i.e., factors believed to be true which, if proved false, can negatively impact the requirements). Example assumptions include availability of software components from libraries, versions of operating systems, and stability of the user's quality attributes.

- Describe any dependencies (i.e., external factors outside the control of the project team that could negatively impact the requirements). An example dependency could be that the requirements depend upon interfaces with the new release of a product or to currently unavailable hardware. If dependencies are already documented in the project plan, refer to the plan document.

- Logically organize the "Functional requirements" section of the template into groups of requirements or features (each briefly described) or into some other useful organization scheme.

- Document quality attributes with their metrics.

- Supplement the SRS document with trace matrices showing the dependencies among requirements.

- Use a template like the one shown below and format the document with the specification information. Identify any document naming and numbering conventions for the SRS document inside the document itself (as shown in section 1.2 in the template).

Software Requirements Specification Template

1. Introduction
   1.1 Purpose
   1.2 Document conventions
   1.3 References
2. Overall description
   2.1 Product overview
   2.2 Product stakeholders and users
   2.3 Product features
   2.4 User documentation
   2.5 Assumptions and dependencies
   2.6 Design and implementation constraints
3. Functional requirements
   3.1 Feature 1
   3.2 Feature 2
   3.3 Feature 3
4. External interface requirements
   4.1 User interfaces
   4.2 Hardware interfaces
   4.3 Software interfaces
5. Quality attributes

Appendices
A: Glossary
B: Analysis models
C: Requirements priority and other attributes
D: Requirements trace matrices

Tip In some change-driven or low-risk projects, analysis models might substitute for functional requirements statements. In such cases, be sure to use multiple detailed analysis models (e.g., scenarios, business rules, logical data models, and state diagrams).

13. Check the SRS document for quality.

- Conduct reviews of the SRS to detect quality issues in the requirements and in the document itself. (See section 6.1 for more information on reviews.) Use an SRS inspection checklist (see an example in Appendix D) to enhance the *inspection* process.

 Tip The quality of the final software product is dependent on excellent requirements. Be sure to apply the information you learned in Chapter 1 on the characteristics of excellent requirements to ensure quality in your SRS.

 Beware! The SRS represents product requirements, not project requirements. It should not include details about the process for producing the software product such as product cost, schedule, reporting, or quality assurance procedures.

Variations

5.2.1 Planguage

Planguage is a language that uses keywords for clear and complete specification of the quality attributes. You can use planguage in place of requirements statements.

Planguage Specification
of Quality Attributes

Tag (Name or label for the requirement)	Performance: QueryResponseTime
Scale (Dimension of measure)	Seconds
Meter (Gauge or measuring device for testing the requirement)	Elapsed time from pressing "Enter" to the complete query response loading onto the screen
Must (Necessary measure to deliver)	• No more than 5 seconds for 98% of queries • No more than 10 seconds for 2% of queries
Plan (Desired measure)	• No more than 3 seconds for 98% of queries • No more than 5 seconds for 2% of queries

[Reference 10: Gilb, 2005]

CHAPTER

6

Validate
the Requirements

Validation assesses whether a product satisfies user needs and conforms to requirements. Requirements validation ensures that the requirements are necessary and sufficiently specified to meet user needs before design and development commences. Requirements validation activities detect and correct any unnecessary and incorrect requirements.

How do I validate requirements?

To validate requirements:

1. **Select and integrate the requirements validation techniques.**

   • Identify which validation techniques will be most effective.

   • Choose a combination of techniques, using different validation techniques for different representations and portions of the requirements.

   • Validate the high-risk requirements early in the process, to reduce overall project risks.

   • Integrate validation activities throughout requirements development.

Validate the Requirements

2. **Ensure adequate user involvement.**

   - Check that user requirements describe how users need to interact with the system. Active user involvement is crucial because validation involves checking conformance to user needs.

   - Have stakeholders check that requirements are complete, consistent, and of high quality, revising the documentation as needed.

   - Ensure that you derive functional requirements from the business and user requirements.

3. **Validate the requirements.**

   - Validate a subset of important requirements early in requirements development. Do not wait until detailed analysis models are completed before checking to see if the right product is being defined.

4. **Revise the requirements documentation.**

   - Revise documentation right away based on validation feedback.

   - Conduct impact analysis if requirements change, to understand how the changes affect project plans.

   - Reprioritize any requirements that change because of validation activities.

   - Repeat the cycle as you progress through the requirements development process.

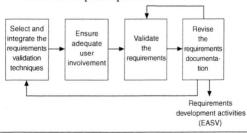

Software Requirements

What Tools and Techniques
Will I Use to Validate Requirements?

When you need to:	Then create:
Review requirements	Peer Reviewed Requirements Documentation
Create validation tests	User Acceptance Tests
Test requirements models	Validated Models
Demonstrate portions of the system	Operational Prototypes

6.1   Peer Review

What is it?

A peer review is a focused meeting in which a small group of stakeholders evaluates requirements documentation or models to find errors and improve quality.

What types of peer reviews are there?

Inspections are the most formal type of peer review. Inspections incorporate the following phases:

- Planning
- Overview meeting
- Individual inspector preparation
- Inspection meeting
- Rework
- Follow-up
- Causal analysis (sometimes, to determine the cause of defects and decide how to prevent defects in future work)

Continued on next page

Inspections also use formal roles (such as moderator, recorder, reader, author, and inspector) and inspection tools (such as inspection procedures, forms, and reports) to capture and report on inspection metrics that will help improve the inspection process itself.

Less-formal peer reviews are also possible. For example, in a *team review*, team members may not capture defect data or perform the follow-up and causal analysis phases. Team reviews also do not typically involve all of the roles defined in formal inspections.

Why do it?

To detect errors and inconsistencies in requirements, to ensure that the requirements adequately represent user needs, to reduce the costs associated with correcting implementation defects that originate in requirements, and to increase software quality.

You can conduct peer reviews on downstream work products (such as tests and code), but peer reviews provide even more value for upstream work products (such as requirements).

What does it do?

- Educates team members (such as developers and testers) about requirements, and ensures that their understanding is consistent with user needs

- Forces analysts to focus validation efforts on those portions of the requirements with the highest risk or ambiguity

- Defines quality expectations for requirements through the creation of inspection or review checklists

---

- Provides a learning environment in which requirements stakeholders can better understand the requirements and business domain

- Identifies requirements process improvement opportunities

How do I do it?

1. **Decide what portions of a requirements work product to review and the type of review approach to conduct.**

   - Identify the requirements documentation to review. Consider user requirements documents, software requirements specification documents, analysis models, and acceptance tests as candidates for review.

   - Determine what portions to review and which type of review to conduct, based on risk. Requirements risk factors to consider include complex business rules, multiple or complex exceptions, complex data states and data dependencies, inexperienced team members, reliance on surrogate users, mission- or safety-critical requirements, and requirements for systems that involve large costs and resources.

   - Use inspections for high-risk portions of requirements, and less-formal reviews for less-risky portions of requirements. Focus your review efforts on those portions of the requirements documentation that have the highest risk.

 Tip Do not wait until you have defined all of the requirements to begin your review. Early reviews of risky requirements can have large paybacks.

2. **Identify the stakeholders who will act as reviewers.**

   - Define who will play which roles when you are using a formal inspection. The author is typically the analyst who produced the items being reviewed. All roles are also inspectors.

- Select people who are requirements consumers (e.g., developers, testers, users, technical and field support, trainers, and developers and analysts of interfacing systems) and requirements providers (e.g., customers, users, product development and marketing representatives, and subject matter experts).

- Limit the total size of the group to no more than seven people.

 Select people who are willing to focus on the issues or defects in the requirements themselves, rather than criticize the person who produced the requirements. In addition, you should select team members who want to participate in inspections and who are willing to have their own work products reviewed.

3. **Plan the review.**

- For formal peer reviews, have the author and moderator (i.e., the person who facilitates the meeting) discuss the author's review goals and decide what portions of the requirements to review. Have them determine what tools (e.g., inspection checklists or supplemental models such as scenarios, state diagrams, and decision tables) will help inspectors prepare for the inspection meeting.

- Schedule the meeting. In more-formal peer reviews, send out the requirements documentation to the inspectors several days prior to the inspection meeting. Be sure that inspectors understand the purpose of the inspection by holding a brief overview meeting or by communicating in writing what the focus of the inspection meeting will be.

- Plan the review meetings realistically. Allow enough time for effective reviews but limit the length of each review meeting to no more than two hours.

Tip As a rule of thumb, you can only inspect two to five pages of a requirements document in a few hours (depending on the document's complexity, format, and content density) so you may need to schedule multiple review meetings.

• Print text-based documents with line numbers to help reviewers quickly locate any issues being raised.

4. **Prepare for the review meeting.**

• Have each inspector (including the author) prepare for an inspection or formal review by spending one to two hours examining the work product. (This is a critical part of the process; most of the errors are detected during individual preparation.)

Tip Individual preparation is critical for effective inspections. If any inspector is not prepared, re-schedule the meeting. Less-formal reviews such as walk-throughs do not rely on individual preparation but focus on educating reviewers, so preparation is less important.

• Use inspection checklists to help inspectors find typical requirements errors. Tailor the checklists to your organization and ask specific inspectors to look for certain defect categories. Have inspectors refer to the checklist multiple times as they examine the requirements. (An example checklist for a software requirements specification is provided in Appendix D.)

• Have each reviewer track how much time he or she spends in preparation, for use in the next step.

5. **Conduct the review.**

• Have the moderator introduce the review and its purpose. Record metrics for each reviewer's preparation time (to use to tailor the process for maximum defect detection. For example, if you

---

find that those reviewers who spent one hour in preparation are the ones who found the most defects, suggest that all reviewers spend an hour in preparation for future reviews.)

- Ask the reader in a more-formal review to paraphrase a small portion of the work product. For less-formal reviews, ask reviewers to make comments about the work product while the recorder or author records the comments.

- Ask reviewers to decide if their comments discuss defects that require follow-up by the author. (Typographical errors are not classified as defects, but are recorded for correction.) Have the recorder capture all information about issues, their severity, their origin, and their location.

- Control discussions and the tendency for participants to solve problems during the peer review meeting. Defer discussions, clarification, and suggestions until after the meeting (unless the peer review can conclude them within a minute or two).

- Decide the disposition of the work product. (It may need to be reworked. In some cases, reviewers will decide to conduct another inspection if the number and severity of errors are too high.)

- Have the moderator lead a discussion for the last five minutes, to debrief the inspection itself. Obtain lessons learned about what worked in the entire process (not just the inspection meeting itself) as well as the results. Use these lessons to adapt inspection practices in the organization.

- Record defect metrics (such as the count and severity of defects) in formal inspections. Follow causal analysis discussions with inspections to explore why and how high-severity defects were injected into the requirements and how to prevent them from being introduced in the future.

6. **Revise the work product based on feedback.**

- Have the author research issues, comments, and defects. Be sure that severe defects are fixed, but allow the author to choose not to correct less-severe defects, as necessary. Have the author track his or her rework time and report it to the recorder or moderator.

- Conduct another inspection or review if necessary.

- Periodically report on aggregate inspection data to detect trends in defects and to modify the inspection process for optimal effectiveness and efficiency.

Variations

6.1.1 Perspective-Based Review

In a perspective-based review, different reviewers (or inspectors, in the case of formal inspections) prepare by reviewing the requirements work product from the point of view of a specific stakeholder (such as a type of user) or provider (such as a tester or designer).

6.2 User Acceptance Tests

What are they?

User acceptance tests are specific test cases that users use to decide whether to accept a delivered system. Each acceptance test is a *black box test* (i.e., a test written without regard to software implementation) that represents the system inputs and the expected results that the final system is designed to execute. During user acceptance testing, users review test results, verify the correctness of the acceptance tests, decide which tests pass or fail, and decide which failed tests are of the highest priority for correction. After testing concludes, users either grant or refuse acceptance of the system.

Alternative names for this technique

- Acceptance Criteria
- Acceptance Tests
- End User Tests
- Functional Tests

Why use it?

To define the conditions for accepting the system, to use these conditions as tests for the requirements, and to allow test activities to begin independently of design and development.

What does it do?

- Guides users to more explicitly describe how they expect the software to work
- Ensures that tests exist to prove the system conforms to customer expectations
- Provides a concrete depiction of the data necessary for users to accept the final system
- Provides a basis for developing user manuals, job aids, or training documentation
- Provides tests useful to model validation

How do I do it?

1. **Define the acceptance criteria for the system.**

    - Identify the functionality, quality attributes, and correct data needed for customers to accept the system (e.g., "the ability to provide a customer waiting on the telephone with an accurate job estimate within thirty seconds" or "each job estimate is within 10% of the final invoice").

    - Ask users, "How will you judge whether the system satisfies your needs?"

Tip User involvement is critical to specifying acceptance criteria. System acceptance criteria are more often based on the user's ability to accomplish specific tasks and the system's ability to meet certain quality attributes, and less often based on meeting a specific end date or a fixed cost for the development effort.

2. Define the acceptance test cases.

 Tip Test cases are the input data and the expected results. Every acceptance criterion should have one or more test cases. Scenarios created during analysis modeling are good sources for test cases.

3. Determine the acceptance test methods.

• Consider using common acceptance testing methods such as:

Method	Explanation
Manual test	Test cases written on paper and walked through the steps manually using analysis models
Graphic user interface (GUI) test tool	Tools that execute the system while recording user actions and the system's responses
Code and test	Code written by developers to run a test, often aided with a testing framework that helps manage the execution of one or more tests
Scripting	Simplified form of code, written by developers or users, that employs a specific notation
Spreadsheet	Spreadsheets created with data values in columns, with an additional column for expected results
Template	A combination of scripts and spreadsheets (Scripts are created to execute tests using the data from the rows in the spreadsheet)

- Determine how each acceptance test will be treated if problems arise during final user acceptance testing. Use this information to focus your validation effort.

4. **Validate the analysis models using the user acceptance tests.**

 Tip Acceptance test failures can have different levels of severity.

Example
Acceptance Test Severity Levels

Severity Level	Definition
1	Critical. It will be impossible to continue with testing or to accept the system because of this error.
2	Major. Testing can continue but the system cannot be deployed with this problem.
3	Medium. Testing can continue and the system is likely to be deployed with some departure from the agreed-upon business functionality.
4	Minor. Testing and deployment can progress. The problem should be corrected but will not impact business functionality.
5	Cosmetic. Errors such as colors, fonts, and interface displays that are less than desirable can be corrected at some future time.

Consider the test's severity level when prioritizing failed tests for correction.

CVGC Example
Acceptance Test Spreadsheet

Input Data

Service Summary	Schedule Date	Contractor Last Name
12 windows – exterior & interior	May 16	Mahoney
16 windows – exterior	April 18	Stewart
Skylight	August 17	Miller
16 windows – exterior & interior; power-wash deck	August 18	Miller
Power-wash deck	August 17	Graham
Skylight; power-wash deck	July 12	Davis

Expected Results for the Test: Search Scheduled Jobs (by Date, Service, or Contractor Last Name)

Query	Records Returned	Comment
July and August	4	Search on date.
Graham	1	Search on contractor name.
Stained glass	0	Search on service. None present. Error message displays: "No records found for search criteria."
Deck or skylight	4	Search on service.

Variations

6.2.1 Draft of the User Manual

Creating a draft of the user manual from the requirements documentation forces a close examination of the requirements and can uncover missing or erroneous requirements. You can use the manual during final systems acceptance testing in situations where the user manual is integral when the system becomes operational.

6.3　Model Validation

What is it?

Model validation uses test simulations (i.e., mock tests rather than real test cases and code) to step through multiple analysis models to uncover missing information and correct documentation errors.

Alternative names for this technique

- Abstract Testing
- Conceptual Testing
- Logical Analysis
- Model Walk-Throughs

Why do it?

To find missing steps, data, and business rules in requirements models and to correct errors in requirements documents.

What does it do?

- Allows users and team members to simulate system operation without actually testing code
- Demonstrates that the models are consistent with one another

---

- Checks that requirements cover typical user situations

- Detects errors, inconsistencies, or missing requirements in analysis models and derived requirements documentation

- Allows a form of testing when a prototype is unavailable or infeasible

How do I do it?

1. **Identify and create the test cases.**

   - Determine one or more sources for the test cases. Consider scenarios or use cases with pre- and post-conditions clearly defined, user acceptance test cases, or test cases devised by users.

   - Modify the test cases as needed, to cover situations that users experience when interacting with the system.

   - Document non-automated test cases in spreadsheets or tables, or use a testing framework to store the test case data to reuse as user acceptance tests.

2. **Select the analysis models to validate.**

   - Select multiple models that cohesively describe the data, rules, and tasks that users will encounter when interacting with the system. For testing software and hardware interfaces, use models that capture triggers, data, and rules.

3. **Trace the test cases through the models in a step-by-step manner.**

   - Manually trace each test case through the models, taking each test from one model to the next. For example, the test case might read, "At the 'schedule job' user interface, the scheduler enters a customer site address of 123 Regency Lane. The last job conducted at that site is displayed." Look for the necessary attributes in the data model and dialog map (e.g., customer address, prior job) and for steps in the use case that describe requesting customer information.

- Walk the tests through the models either individually or in small groups. (If using small groups, paraphrase what is occurring to help detect errors.) Have participants raise questions and issues throughout the process.

- Look for errors in the models, including moving to the wrong screens and missing or extraneous steps, business rules, events, and data.

4. **Correct the requirements models.**

- Adjust the models and repeat the testing process.

- Correct all requirements documentation derived from the models.

6.4 *Operational Prototype*

What is it?

An operational prototype is a prototype built to demonstrate that the system can satisfy user needs. Unlike exploratory prototypes that clarify ambiguous requirements, operational prototypes test the feasibility of portions of the system, implement functionality for which user satisfaction is uncertain, or permit users to check whether an aspect of the quality attributes can be satisfied. Operational prototypes are useful to minimize the risks associated with large, complex systems or to provide a reusable basis for incremental software deployment.

Alternative names for this technique

- Demonstration
- Proof of Concept
- Structural Prototype
- Vertical Prototype

Why use it?

To demonstrate how a portion of the software will work once it is operational, to demonstrate whether known requirements will satisfy customers, and to validate external interface requirements.

What does it do?

- Assesses the feasibility of quality attributes such as performance, usability, or security
- Detects unnecessary functionality, missing steps, or overly complex user interfaces that could inhibit meeting user needs
- Tests complex or risky interfaces to external hardware or software components
- Permits developers to obtain design and development experience early in the project
- Reduces overall project risk by revealing missing, erroneous, and infeasible requirements

How do I do it?

1. **Determine which requirements to validate using an operational prototype.**

    - Select requirements that pose risks (such as requirements that may not be feasible, complex business rules, or algorithms) or needs that pose critical usability requirements. Choose high-priority

---

use cases or scenarios when validating usability or critical functional requirements.

- Be sure the selected requirements are well understood.

2. **Develop the prototype.**

- Decide between developing a throwaway or evolutionary prototype. (A throwaway is generally quicker to build but is ultimately discarded. An evolutionary prototype requires skilled developers and more effort but can evolve into a deliverable product.)

- Use real data and user-defined scenarios.

- Build the prototype iteratively (i.e., develop a small prototype to begin with, evaluate it with users, and then revise it as needed before adding more functionality).

3. **Evaluate the prototype.**

- Identify users to test the prototype. Be sure to clarify the purpose of the prototype with users before you begin.

- Conduct a demonstration. For prototypes of user interfaces, have users try to use the operational prototype. Ask them to use scenarios or tasks (from user task analysis) to guide their tests.

- Ask prepared questions such as "Does this next step make sense?" "Is the response time sufficient?" "What slows you down?" and "Do the messages make sense?"

- Run a test of the built portion of the system for prototypes that involve an exchange of signals or data between software or hardware components, to test performance or a complex algorithm.

- Record issues that surface during the evaluation. Revise the requirements documentation and prototype to reflect necessary changes.

Operational prototypes are not useful when requirements are not feasible to test or to simulate, such as those that address safety or conditions that are not reproducible in a partial solution (e.g., missile launch, space module landing, nuclear waste detection).

Variations

6.4.1 Usability Tests

You can conduct operational prototype usage trials in a usability test to record, observe, and analyze what happens when users try to accomplish tasks with operational prototypes. Usability tests (also called usability labs or usability analysis) assess user experience when interacting with the software. They are controlled environments in which users operate a prototype version of the system. Data about user interactions is collected and analyzed, often by using software to record each user interaction (i.e., the number of user errors or restarts, the number of keystrokes or clicks (or the clock time) needed to complete a task, the number and percentage of planned tasks that were completed, or any screens, dialogs, or steps not completed or used).

Follow usability tests with interviews or surveys to learn users' subjective reactions to the prototype. Use this data to adjust the prototype and requirements for increased usability and performance.

When Should I Use Specific Requirements Validation Techniques?

Validation Technique	Use When:
Peer reviews	• The right mix of reviewers is available to participate. • The team culture encourages giving feedback to increase quality. • Reviews can be integrated early into requirements development.
User acceptance tests	• Users are willing and available to develop tests. • User acceptance tests will be saved for final system testing.
Model validation	• The requirements models exist. • Tests can be devised by the analyst, the users, or a combination.
Operational protoypes	• User expectations can be managed (e.g., they understand that the prototype is not the finished system). • Developers are available and trained to use the prototyping tool. • The target requirements are feasible for prototyping.

CHAPTER
7

Manage the Requirements

Software requirements are often not stable and fixed, but may change because of numerous factors such as mistakes or oversights during elicitation, the evolving nature of understanding complex systems, emerging technology, changing business or regulatory demands, and competitive pressures. Improper management of changing requirements are often a source of project delays and overruns.

Requirements management is the process of monitoring the status of requirements and controlling changes to the requirements baseline. Requirements management is a full life-cycle activity, beginning as you develop requirements and continuing throughout software development. To manage requirements, you need to establish procedures that will enable your team to quickly understand the impact of changes, decide how to deal with changing requirements, and renegotiate requirements commitments.

What Tools and Techniques Will I Use to Manage Requirements?

When you need to:	Then create:
Establish mechanisms for managing changing requirements	Change Control Policies and Procedures
Identify supplemental requirements information	Requirements Attributes
Understand requirements lineage and relationships	Requirements Trace Matrices

7.1 Change Control Policies and Procedures

What are they?

Change control policies and procedures establish mechanisms and rules for recognizing, evaluating, and deciding how to integrate new and evolving requirements into the requirements baseline.

Why do it?

To anticipate and respond to changing requirements, to establish efficient procedures that allow for legitimate changes to requirements while minimizing disruption to project plans, and to make the most effective use of stakeholders' time for evaluating and resolving changes.

What does it do?

- Aligns the software project with changing business needs

- Ensures that customers understand and accept requirements changes

- Defines what and how requirements changes will be recorded

- Establishes procedures for understanding what requirements and development deliverables are associated with changing requirements, to assist with impact analysis

- Schedules requirements for implementation or deferral

How do I do it?

1. **Identify the change control procedures.**

   - Include procedures for:

     - Proposing requirements changes.

     - Conducting impact analysis.

     - Evaluating trade-offs posed by requirements changes.

     - Making decisions about proposed requirements changes.

     - Updating requirements documents.

     - Monitoring requirements volatility.

- Include requirements change monitoring practices such as requirements version control and status reporting. Define version control guidelines such as how requirements documentation will be identified and circumstances when versions will be updated. Describe the guidelines for status reporting (including timing, recipients, and report contents).

- Describe the allowable statuses for requirements and the rules for status transitions. (Example statuses include proposed, approved, deferred, scheduled, and implemented.)

- Identify who should be notified of changed requirements and the circumstances under which they should be notified.

- Keep the change control procedures simple. Define short turnaround times for each step and decide how you will notify requestors about the disposition of change requests.

 Consider using robust *requirements management tools* to manage requirements changes in large projects. Requirements management tools store requirements information in a database, capture requirements attributes and associations, and facilitate requirements management reporting. Some tools also have interfaces with change control and testing tools. (See www.ebgconsulting.com/requirementresources.php for a list of requirements management tools.)

Use less-formal tools (e.g., a spreadsheet or a simple database) for requirements management on smaller projects or in organizations not yet ready to adapt a more-powerful software tool.

 Record rejected requirements and the rationale for their rejection. (The rejected requirements might be proposed again.)

Tip Identify and monitor volatile requirements (i.e., those that change frequently). Changes to volatile requirements may be legitimate (e.g., changing regulations, emergent business needs, evolving market demands). Developers may be able to design the system to minimize the downstream impact of volatile requirements.

2. **Create a *change control board (CCB).***

- Identify the change control roles and responsibilities for a small group of stakeholders who will make decisions on the disposition and treatment of changing requirements. Typical roles include a chairperson (who receives requirements change requests, and calls and facilitates meetings), evaluators (who consider the impact of the changes), and verifiers (who confirm the impact analysis and business importance).

- Include a balance of business and technical staff. Keep the group small (under ten members, if possible). If larger projects require more members, be sure that the group has strong leadership, well-planned and well-facilitated meetings, and strict turnaround guidelines.

- Include participants who can decide on the disposition of each proposed requirements change. (CCB members must be able to consider issues such as cost and schedule impact of requirements changes, requirements priorities, and the coordination of multiple changes.)

- Identify and communicate how the CCB will make decisions. Be sure all team members and project stakeholders understand the decision process. Share the rationale for decisions with all project stakeholders.

Process Map Showing Requirements Change Control Procedures

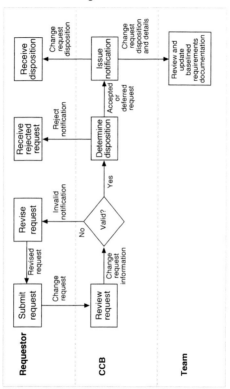

3. **Create a baseline for the requirements.**

   • Uniquely identify each requirement. Be sure that you
     record all necessary requirements attributes. (See the

next section in this chapter for more information on requirements attributes.) Use a requirements management tool to record all of the requirements information.

4. **Begin implementing your change control process once you have created a requirements baseline. Be sure to report and monitor any changes.**

Use informal change control processes for smaller, less-risky projects. One approach is to have the team work on a small set of requirements for a few weeks to deliver an increment of the system's functionality. For each increment, have the team explore and prioritize requirements, develop tests, design and implement code, and present the product to customers and users for evaluation and acceptance. Ask business and technical staff to act as a change control board, deciding which requirements to develop for the next increment, and give the business product champion the final authority on requirements decisions.

Typically, change control is managed during each increment by saying "no" (i.e., no changes are allowed to the requirements), although requirements change requests should be recorded in a requirements backlog for review at the start of the next increment.

Change Request Identification	Requirements Identification	Brief Description	Request Date	Disposition	Disposition Date	Disposition Rationale
CR-3	EST.BID-2.0	The system shall provide contractors with the ability to bid on outstanding jobs.	June 9	Deferred	June 11	Depends on multi-company support and adds technical complexity and risk. Primary goals for streamlined operations must be achieved first.
CR-6	QRY.JOB-1.0	The system shall provide the capability for customers to view their invoice.	June 10	Rejected	June 11	Little or no business benefit (e.g. increased revenue, streamlined operations) is gained from this capability.

7.2   Requirements Attributes

What are they?
Requirements attributes are supplemental information associated with requirements.

Why do it?
To collect information useful for explaining, justifying, tracing, and reporting on requirements.

What does it do?
- Gives stakeholders useful information for filtering, selecting, and analyzing requirements
- Provides information to change control decision makers about the impact of changing requirements
- Helps to educate new team members about the requirements
- Provides historical information about requirements that helps teams maintain or enhance delivered software

How do I do it?
1. **Identify the attributes that you need to track.**
   - Select only the necessary and sufficient attributes for the project. Be judicious when picking attributes because capturing and monitoring requirements information requires team time and effort.
   - Consider project history, team or organizational culture, and the nature of the requirements when selecting attributes. (For example, if there are many regulatory requirements, document a "source" attribute that identifies the people, documents, or regulatory bodies from which the requirements originated.)

Example Requirements
Attributes and Descriptions

Attribute	Explanation
Rationale	Purpose for the requirement
Priority	Relative importance of the requirement (e.g., must, should, could, etc.)
Status	Current state of the requirement (e.g., proposed, approved, tested, deferred, rejected)
Status date	Date that the requirement was assigned the current status
Owner	Area or person responsible for verifying and approving that the requirement is correct and tested
Source	Origin of the requirement (e.g., regulation, customer, derived from other requirements)
Supporting material	References to other documents (e.g., regulations, standards, user manuals)
Complexity	Degree of complexity of the requirement (e.g., high, medium, low)
Volatility	Degree of change that the requirement is likely to experience as it is being implemented (e.g., high, medium, low)

2. **Define and maintain attributes for all requirements.**

   • Select attributes to track as you initially create the requirements baseline and maintain these attributes throughout the project. Include the same attributes for all new or modified requirements.

Consider using a requirements management tool to assist in capturing, filtering, and reporting on requirements by their attributes.

Example Requirements Attributes Matrix

Requirements Identification	Requirements Attributes				
	Features or Quality Attribute Name	Priority	Status	Status Date	Planned Release
SCH-3.2	Scheduling	Must	Approved	Feb 7	R1
CON-1.1	Contractor maintenance	Should	Reviewing	Jan 31	R2
QRY-2.3	Query	Could	Deferred	Feb 14	R2
SEC-1.0	Security	Must	Approved	Feb 11	R1

7.3 Requirements Trace Matrices

What is it?

A requirements trace matrix (RTM) identifies how requirements are related to software development deliverables and to other requirements. Requirements matrices show related requirements and the forward and backward lineage to project deliverables.

Requirements Tracing

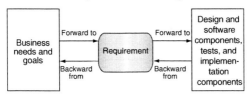

Why do it?

To understand how requirements changes impact other requirements and downstream software development deliverables.

What does it do?

• Shows interdependencies among requirements

- Gives management insight into the status of the development effort by identifying what development deliverables exist to satisfy requirements

- Provides reports that are useful for monitoring contract compliance

- Demonstrates when requirements have been satisfied by associating them to system components and tests

- Helps maintainers identify the software deliverables affected by the requirements being modified

How do I do it?

1. **Determine which software development deliverables to trace.**

    - Trace related requirements such as use cases, business rules, features, functional requirements, and quality requirements.

    - Trace requirements to downstream development deliverables such as design components, source code files, test cases or scripts (e.g., system, integration, and acceptance tests), and implementation deliverables (e.g., user manuals, training guides, and support procedures).

    - Select requirements for tracing that can ease impact analysis. (For example, if you develop use cases and business rules during requirements analysis and there are a large number of volatile business rules associated with each use case, trace business rules to use cases. This will enable your team to quickly identify use cases affected by changing business rules.)

    - Select only those downstream elements that are necessary and sufficient to verify that requirements have been properly designed and tested.

 Tip   Tracing requirements has a long-term payback because it facilitates software maintenance and

---

enhancement. Software maintainers can look at requirements trace matrices to identify the design, code, and test deliverables that need to be modified for a particular requirements change.

2. Create the requirements trace matrices.

- Track requirements relationships by recording the requirements information and associated project or software development deliverables in the columns of the matrices.

- Educate team members about the matrices and be sure to keep the source information that you store in it current.

- Update the matrices continually throughout the project and use them to report on the status of the project.

Requirements management tools are useful when teams are familiar with the discipline of managing requirements. They can be very complex to use and require training. The tools do not manage the requirements; people do. Be sure that requirements management procedures are effective and are being practiced before implementing an automated requirements management tool. Assign one team member (and a backup person) with the primary responsibility to learn and use the requirements management tool.

Requirement Identification	Use Case			
	UC1	UC2	UC3	UC4
SCH-3.2	↵			
EST-3.2			↵	
CLO-2.3		↵		↵

RTM During Requirements Development, Showing Functional Requirements Derived From Use Cases

RTM as Software Development Proceeds

Requirement		Design Elements		Code	System Tests	Acceptance Test	
Requirement Identification		Package Identification	Version Number	Module	Script	Test Case(s)	Acceptance Test Date
SCH-1.2		DE-436	2.3	CVSC9897	SSCVSC01	ACTSC421	Sep 17
					SSCVSC08	ACTSC429	Sep 19
SEC-1.0		DE-887	1.4	LBR903	SSSR9	ACTSR01	Sep 10

CHAPTER 8

Adapting Requirements Practices to Projects

There are variety of techniques, team processes, and documentation styles to choose from as you develop and manage your requirements. Because every software project is different, you need to adapt your practices based on two considerations: 1) the type of project and 2) whether the project is change-driven or risk-driven.

Project types

It is important to consider project type before adapting your requirements practices and selecting analysis models. Projects are typically classified into three main categories:

Types of Software Development Projects

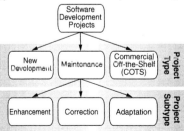

Software Development Project Types

Project Type:
New development

Other Names:
Greenfield development, custom development

Goal:
To create a new software product

Requirements Adaptations:
Assess requirements factors to determine whether you should use risk-driven or change-driven practices. (See the next section in this chapter for more information on risk-driven and change-driven practices.)

Chief Concerns:
Balancing correct and complete requirements documentation with flexibility and speed. If development is to be contracted to an outside organization, more requirements documentation is necessary for effective requirements.

Suggested Analysis Models and Requirements-Related Documentation:
- Product scope models (e.g., vision statement, context diagram, event-response table, glossary)
- A subset of analysis models to specify functional requirements (e.g., actor table, use cases, business rules, and data model)
- Quality attributes, design constraints, and external interfaces

Software Development Project Types, cont.

Project Type:
  Enhancement (Maintenance)

Other Names:
  Continuing engineering

Goal:
  To add functionality to an existing software product

Requirements Adaptations:
  - Create a minimal set of requirements for the current ("as-is") system using existing systems documentation, develop a rich set of "to-be" requirements, and then perform gap analysis to determine what to change.
  - Refer to requirements trace matrices to locate the design and code deliverables that need to change and to locate reusable test cases. Update requirements documentation to facilitate future enhancements.

Chief Concerns:
  Using existing systems documentation that is not reliable

Suggested Analysis Models and Requirements-Related Documentation:
  For the "as-is" system:
  - Context diagram
  - Actor table
  - Data model
  - Use cases (brief description only), scenarios, or both
  - Use case map
  - Business rules

  For the "to-be" system:
  - Context diagram or events (if the "to-be" model is different from the "as-is" model)
  - Actor table (if the "to-be" model is different)
  - Data model or data dictionary (to identify any new data)
  - Use cases, scenarios, or both (for new or enhanced use cases)
  - Use case map (if the "to-be" model is different)
  - Business rules (any new or changed rules)
  - Quality attributes (e.g., usability, performance, and security)
  - Any new external interfaces and design constraints

Software Development Project Types, cont.

Project Type:
Correction (Maintenance)

Other Names:
Maintenance; fix; defect correction

Goal:
To fix problems affecting the quality or correctness
of existing software

Requirements Adaptations:
- Reduce the risk of introducing errors in existing software by
  defining user acceptance tests at the same time as you
  identify functional and quality attributes.
- Refer to requirements trace matrices to locate the design
  and code deliverables to change, and to find reusable
  test cases.
- Create a minimal amount of requirements documentation
  (just enough to help future correction activities).

Chief Concerns:
Introducing new errors with each change to existing software

**Suggested Analysis Models and
Requirements-Related Documentation:**
Revise (if any of these requirements exist) or create:
- Business rules
- Data model or data dictionary
- Use cases or scenarios
- User acceptance test cases
- Quality attributes

Project Type:

Adaptation (Maintenance)

Other Names:

Technical migration

Goal:

To move existing software to a new technical environment

Requirements Adaptations:

• Define acceptance test cases, including the acceptance criteria for the adapted system.
• Identify a strategy for transitioning to the new operational environment.

Chief Concerns:

Not losing existing functionality, business capability, or expected service levels (i.e., performance, security, reliability, or other quality attributes)

Suggested Analysis Models and Requirements-Related Documentation:

• Performance, usability, and other quality attributes
• External interfaces
• Use cases (brief descriptions) or functional requirements text

Software Development Project Types, cont.

Project Type:
Commercial off-the-shelf (COTS) software

Other Names:
Packaged solution; software package; vendor components

Goal:
To replace existing software, business processes, or both by aquiring existing software components rather than developing new components

Requirements Adaptations:
- Use operational prototypes to generate test cases for product evaluation.
- Define requirements such that user acceptance test cases can be easily documented (for example, by developing use cases, scenarios, or both).
- Document the "as-is" and "to-be" business processes that need to change.
- Define functional requirements at a high level, as named features.
- Be sure the COTS solution's business rules are configurable to comply with corporate policies, industry standards, or government regulations. (Business rules are critical to define because the COTS business rules are likely to need tailoring.)
- Compare the COTS data model with your conceptual data model to find the closest fit. Identify gaps in data and structural business rules.
- Satisfy the necessary quality attributes. (Satisfying quality attributes is as critical as satisfying the required functional requirements.)

Chief Concerns:
Selecting and installing a COTS solution that meets user needs, perhaps with some configuration or customization. Well-defined requirements are essential to evaluating and choosing the COTS solution. Understanding business processes that need to change is crucial for implementation and user adoption.

***Suggested Analysis Models and
Requirements-Related Documentation:***

- Process map
- Actor table or map
- Summary-level functional requirements text or use cases (brief descriptions)
- Scenarios
- Business rules
- Data model
- User acceptance tests
- Quality attributes (e.g., performance, security, interoperability, flexibility, and usability)

Change-driven vs. risk-driven projects

You can broadly categorize software projects as *risk-driven* or *change-driven*.

Risk-driven projects tend to be critical systems (i.e., those in which failures are business-, mission-, or safety-critical). They often have fairly stable requirements and require large teams, some of which may be geographically distributed.

Change-driven projects tend toward developing or acquiring software that poses less risk and complexity. These projects have more-volatile requirements and smaller teams (often physically collocated).

(In practice, most projects fall somewhere along a gradient between these extremes.)
[Reference 11: Boehm and Turner, 2004]

Why do it?

To plan and conduct "just enough" requirements development and management for a specific software project.

What does it do?

Examines project factors, for any type of project, to adapt requirements practices (i.e., amount and formality of documentation, use of analysis models, elicitation and validation techniques to draw upon, definition of requirements-related roles and responsibilities, and practices for ongoing process improvement)

Key questions to ask

- Who are the consumers of the requirements?
- What will the requirements be used for?
- Where does this project fall in the range of factors that characterize a project?

How do I do it?

1. **Evaluate the project characteristics.**

   • Characterize the project as risk-driven (e.g., plan-driven or prescriptive) or change-driven (e.g., agile, adaptive, or dynamic) by reviewing the:

   - Application criticality, complexity, and size.

   - Requirements stability.

   - Documentation usage.

   - User involvement.

   - Team, organization, and culture.

	Risk-Driven Projects	Change-Driven Projects
Application Criticality, Complexity, and Size	Requirements are mission-, safety-, or financially critical. Software failure can risk lives, the mission, business success, or financial vitality. The software may be based on many complex rules and have multiple interfacing components.	Requirements are dynamic, emergent, or business-volatile (e.g., e-commerce, financial, or consumer products with short life cycles) with small-to-medium application size and complexity. The software will affect the bottom line but will not put the organization out of business or affect human survival.
Requirements Stability	Requirements are determinable in advance and are relatively stable once elicited. There are many requirements needing organization and prioritization. Large groups of interrelated requirements must be implemented at the same time.	Requirements are turbulent and undergo continual change. It is more business-critical to respond to changing requirements than to adhere to formal plans. A subset of requirements can be elicited and analyzed in small chunks. Informal reviews and user acceptance tests are useful for requirements validation.

Continued on next page

	Risk-Driven Projects	**Change-Driven Projects**
Documentation Usage	Documentation is used to estimate, design, maintain, train new staff, or provide regulatory compliance. Documentation is shared with external organizations (including outsourced organizations) and a dispersed user community.	Documentation is used for developing exploratory prototypes or small increments of the system. There is greater reliance on face-to-face communication. Documentation is primarily used internally.
User Involvement	User involvement is formally managed and requirements elicitation reporting is ongoing. Formality in written documentation is often driven by the contractual nature of the project, part-time availability of users and advisors, their physical dispersion, or a combination.	Users are collocated with technical staff and are available for face-to-face informal meetings.
Team, Organization, and Culture	Project may have one or more distributed teams, each of which tends to be large (e.g., twelve or more). Teams include a mix of new and experienced team members interacting with users dispersed around the country or world who represent diverse needs that require careful negotiation.	Project includes collocated or small teams (e.g., seven or less) that collaborate daily or weekly. Most team members are experienced and highly skilled.

2. **Select the elicitation techniques, analysis models, requirements validation techniques, and management practices for the project.**

   - Determine the project type (see the previous section in this chapter for more information on project types) for requirements adaptations and suggested analysis models.

   - Choose models that fit the business problem domain. (See "How do I choose the right models?" in Chapter 4.)

   - Decide how much detail you need to adequately represent each model. (Risk-driven projects will need multiple models with more detail to find missing or incorrect requirements.)

   - Choose one or more validation techniques (i.e., operational prototypes, user acceptance tests, model validation, and inspections and reviews). Risk-driven projects rely on a combination of techniques, whereas change-driven projects rely primarily on user acceptance tests.

   - Identify the requirements attributes to track, how you will control change, and what to trace.

   - Establish a *timebox* (i.e., a fixed period of time to accomplish the desired outcome) for delivering requirements. Within the overall timebox, plan to develop requirements in three to four iterations, each with its own timebox. For each timebox, decide what specific requirements documentation you should complete, what degree of detail you will need, and how the team will know whether the requirements documentation is acceptable at the end of the iteration or not.

Risk-driven projects tend toward longer requirements iterations (i.e., one month or longer). Change-driven projects tend toward shorter iterations of days or weeks.

- Use a combination of practices for projects that are a hybrid of both change-driven and risk-driven characteristics.

3. **Determine the necessary requirements work products.**

 Work products include vision, stakeholder categories and involvement strategy, scope and analysis models, documentation templates, documented validation plans and procedures, and requirements management documentation and tools.

- Include business models if significant business process or policy changes are anticipated or if a COTS solution is planned.

- Choose analysis models based on the project type. (Refer to the "Project types" section in this chapter for suggested analysis models to use.)

- Be aware that the amount of formal requirements processes and documentation increases with the system's complexity, size, and criticality.

 For risk-driven projects, ask, "Is it riskier to leave *in* or to leave *out* a process or document?" and plan accordingly. For change-driven projects, assume requirements work products are not needed unless there is a compelling reason to include them (for example, because an external agency needs them).

- As a general rule, tailor your practices as follows:

	For Risk-Driven Projects	**For Change-Driven Projects**
Amount of Documentation	Develop multiple documents and share them with a large community of analysts and users. The software needs to be integrated into larger systems, as the overall system is composed of multiple subsystems of software, hardware, and human systems. Formal baselines are created for requirements, and specification documentation strives to be complete, consistent, traceable, and testable.	Develop working software in short (one- to four-week) iterations with minimal requirements documentation.
Use of Analysis Models	Use several detailed models that are verified against each other for higher quality requirements models.	Continually reprioritize requirements and represent them informally using stories or scenarios.
Elicitation and Validation Techniques	Combine interviews, facilitated workshops, and focus groups. Use inspections and operational prototypes for requirements validation.	Use exploratory prototypes; multiple, short facilitated workshops; informal interviews; and user acceptance tests.

- Review user requirements and software requirement specifications formats (or templates) and select the portions that are necessary to formally document.

4. **Determine requirements roles and responsibilities.**

  • Train team members on requirements development and management practices and identify who will be responsible for requirements development and management activities. Be sure everyone understands the rationale for all of the requirements practices.

  • Identify who will create the requirements deliverables (e.g., the product vision, stakeholder profiles and inclusion strategy, and requirements documents) and who will be involved in requirements elicitation.

  • Include business customers as you make decisions about who will participate in requirements development and which business managers will participate in requirements change control activities.

  • Gather the team in meetings to clarify these details. Review all planned requirements practices as a team. Evaluate your approach, checking to ensure that it incorporates good practices.

 Review for the following good requirements practices and adapt them to your risk-driven or change-driven project.

Good Requirements
Development and Management Practices

Good requirements have:

❑ A clear vision
❑ A clearly defined product scope
❑ A well-defined stakeholder elicitation plan
❑ A combination of multiple requirements elicitation techniques
❑ Requirements developed in an iterative manner
❑ Combined text and visual analysis models
❑ Requirements reviews conducted
❑ Prioritized requirements
❑ Completed baseline and tracking requirements
❑ Identified and executed change control practices
❑ Well-defined requirements development and management roles and responsibilities
❑ Documented requirements practices and requirements documentation templates
❑ Requirements development retrospectives conducted

 Tip
Risk-driven projects should formalize roles and responsibilities for requirements deliverables and processes. The team can use a worksheet (like the one on the following page) to formally document roles and responsibilities.

Sample Requirements
Roles and Responsibilities Worksheet

	Roles and Responsibilities
Requirements Deliverable or Process	Use cases
Purpose	To define user requirements and provide a basis for identifying business rules and data requirements
Producer(s)	Harry Foot, Analyst
Owner	Marsha Saransky, CVGC Scheduler
Approvers	Paul Deer, Office Manager; Jerry Adams, Bookkeeper
Reviewers	Seth Lee, Estimator/Scheduler; Jamal Quick, Callback Liaison; Harry Foot, Analyst; Amy Table, Database Administrator; Trish Faith, Project Manager
Format or Tool	WordProcessBlue document
Entry Criteria (Dependencies)	• Vision statement • Agreed-upon scope (in the form of a context diagram and event-response table) • Named use cases and scenarios for each use case (optionally, a preliminary list of actors) • Agreed-upon template for documenting use cases
Exit Criteria (How We Know It's Complete)	Scenario walk-throughs of each use case yield no further corrections to the use cases.

5. **Conduct requirements retrospectives.**

   • Continually assess your requirements development and management practices once requirements activities begin, by periodically stopping work to examine requirements practices and deliverables in short requirements retrospectives.

- Have the team identify requirements practices that work, those that do not work, learning points, and suggestions for adapting practices, before continuing with the next iteration of requirements development.

Requirements retrospectives should be well structured and last several hours. (The length will depend on the time frame being reviewed, quantity of work, and the number of participants).

- Hold requirements retrospectives immediately after completing each requirements iteration. Include all of the people who participated in the iteration or delivery period being reviewed.

Retrospectives are one of the most efficient ways for teams to acquire and use knowledge. Use retrospectives regularly; not only during requirements development but also at the end of any important project milestone or iteration and at the end of the project. By using retrospectives during requirements development, the team can learn good practices, avoid faulty decisions or practices, and prepare for their next activity together. General questions to ask during any retrospectives include:

- What is working well that we want to continue doing?
- What can be improved?
- What surprises us?
- What puzzles us?

For specific questions to explore during a requirements retrospective, see "Questions for Requirements Retrospectives" in Appendix G.

Appendix A: References, Bibliography, and Additional Resources

References

1. Moore, Geoffrey A. 1999. *Crossing the Chasm: Marketing and Selling High-Tech Products to Mainstream Customers (Revised Edition)*. HarperCollins Publishers.

2. Beyer, Hugh and Karen Holtzblatt. 1998. *Contextual Inquiry: Defining Customer-Centered Systems*. Morgan Kaufman Publishers, Inc.

3. Gause, Donald C. and Gerald M. Weinberg. 1989. *Exploring Requirements: Quality Before Design*. Dorset House Publishing.

4. Gottesdiener, Ellen. 2002. *Requirements by Collaboration: Workshops for Defining Needs*. Addison-Wesley.

5. Pardee, William J. 1996. *To Satisfy & Delight Your Customer*. Dorset House.

6. Smith, Larry W. December 2000. "Project Clarity through Stakeholder Analysis," *Crosstalk* 13(2): 4-9.

7. Stapleton, Jennifer. 1997. *DSDM: Dynamic Systems Development Method*. Addison-Wesley.

8. Wiegers, Karl. 2003. *Software Requirements (Second Edition)*. Microsoft Press.

9. Ambler, Scott. 2005. *The Elements of UML™ 2.0 Style*. Cambridge University Press.

10. Gilb, Tom. 2005. *Competitive Engineering: A Handbook For Systems Engineering, Requirements Engineering, and Software Engineering Using Planguage*. Elsevier Butterworth-Heinemann.

11. Boehm, Barry and Richard Turner. 2004. *Balancing Agility and Discipline: A Guide for the Perplexed*. Addison-Wesley.

Bibliography

For additional information on:	Refer to:
Requirements Development and Management	• Hooks, Ivy F. and Kristina A. Farry. 2001. *Customer-Centered Products: Creating Successful Products Through Smart Requirements Management*. AMACOM. • Kovitz, Benjamin. 1998. *Practical Software Requirements*. Manning Publications Company. • Lauesen, Soren. 2002. *Software Requirements: Styles and Techniques*. Addison-Wesley. • Robertson, Suzanne and James Robertson. 1999. *Mastering the Requirements Process*. Addison-Wesley. • Sommerville, Ian and Peter Sawyer. 1997. *Requirements Engineering: A Good Practice Guide*. John Wiley & Sons. • Stevens, Richard, Peter Brook, Ken Jackson, and Stuart Arnold. 1998. *Systems Engineering: Coping with Complexity*. Prentice Hall Europe. • Thayer, Richard H. and Merlin Dorfman. 1997. *Software Requirements Engineering (Second Edition)*. IEEE Computer Society Press. • Wiegers, Karl E. 2003. *Software Requirements (Second Edition)*. Microsoft Press.
Elicitation	• Smith, Larry W. December 2000. "Project Clarity through Stakeholder Analysis," *Crosstalk* 13(2): 4-9. • Beyer, Hugh and Karen Holtzblatt. 1998. *Contextual Inquiry: Defining Customer-Centered Systems*. Morgan Kaufman Publishers, Inc. • Gause, Donald C. and Gerald M. Weinberg. 1989. *Exploring Requirements: Quality Before Design*. Dorset House Publishing. • Gottesdiener, Ellen. 2002. *Requirements by Collaboration: Workshops for Defining Needs*. Addison-Wesley.
Analysis (Including Prioritization)	• Cockburn, Alistair. 2000. *Writing Effective Use Cases*. Addison-Wesley. • Cohn, Mike. 2004. *User Stories Applied: For Agile Software Development*. Addison-Wesley.

Continued on next page

For additional information on:	Refer to:
Analysis (continued)	• Constantine, Larry L. and Lucy A.D. Lockwood. 1999. *Software for Use: A Practical Guide to the Models and Methods of Usage-Centered Design*. Addison-Wesley. • Damelio, Robert. 1996. *The Basics of Process Mapping*. Productivity Inc. • Davis, Alan. 1993. *Software Requirements: Objects, Functions, and States (Second Edition)*. PTR Prentice Hall. • Davis, Alan M. March 2003. "The Art of Requirements Triage," *IEEE Computer* 36(3): 42-49. • Ginn, Dana and Evelyn Varner. 2004. *The Design for Six Sigma Memory Jogger™*. GOAL/QPC. • Herzwurm, Georg, Sixten Schockert, and Werner Mellis. 2000. *Joint Requirements Engineering: QFD for Rapid Customer-Focused Software and Internet-Development*. Frieder. Vieweg & Sohn. • Kulak, Daryl and Eamonn Guiney. 2003. *Use Cases: Requirements in Context (Second Edition)*. Addison-Wesley. • Leffingwell, Dean and Don Widrig. 1999. *Managing Software Requirements: A Unified Approach*. Addison-Wesley. • McGraw, Karen L. Karan Harbison. 1997. *User-Centered Requirements: The Scenario-Based Engineering Process*. Lawrence Erlbaum Associates, Inc. • McMenamin, Stephen M. and John Palmer. 1984. *Essential Systems Analysis*. Yourdon, Inc. • Pardee, William J. 1996. *To Satisfy & Delight Your Customer*. Dorset House. • Ross, Ronald G. 1998. *Business Rule Concepts*. Database Research Group. • Rummler, Geary A. and Alan P. Brache. 1990. *Improving Performance: How to Manage the White Space on the Organization Chart*. Jossey-Bass. • Simsion, Graeme. 2000. *Data Modeling Essentials (Second Edition): A Comprehensive Guide to Data Analysis, Design, and Innovation*. Coriolis Group Books.

Continued on next page

For additional information on:	Refer to:
Specification	• Alexander, Ian F. and Richard Stevens. 2002. *Writing Better Requirements*. Addison-Wesley. • Gilb, Tom. 2005. *Competitive Engineering: A Handbook For Systems Engineering, Requirements Engineering, and Software Engineering Using Planguage*. Elsevier Butterworth-Heinemann.
Validation	• Davis, Alan. September 1992. "Operational Prototyping: A New Development Approach," *IEEE Software* 9(5): 70-78. • Freedman, Daniel P. and Gerald M. Weinberg. 1990. *Handbook of Walkthroughs, Inspections, and Technical Reviews*. Dorset House Publishing. • Wiegers, Karl E. 2001. *Peer Reviews in Software: A Practical Guide*. Addison-Wesley.
Requirements Management	• Jarke, Matthias. December 1998. "Requirements Tracing," *Communications of the ACM* 41(12): 32-46. • Davis, Alan L. and Dean Leffingwell. April 1999. "Making Requirements Management Work for You," *Crosstalk* 12(4): 10-13.
Adapting Requirements Practices	• Boehm, Barry and Richard Turner. 2004. *Balancing Agility and Discipline: A Guide for the Perplexed*. Addison-Wesley. • Boehm, Barry. July 2000. "Requirements that Handle IKIWISI, COTS and Rapid Change," *IEEE Computer* 33(7): 99-102. • Kerth, Norman L. 2001. *Project Retrospectives: A Handbook for Team Reviews*. Dorset House. • Young, Ralph R. 2001. *Effective Requirements Practices*. Addison-Wesley.

Additional Resources

IEEE

- *www.swebok.org*

  The Institute of Electrical and Electronic Engineers (IEEE) *Software Engineering Body of Knowledge: Software Requirements Engineering Knowledge Area* (see section on software requirements)

- IEEE good practice guidelines for user (concept of operations), software, and system standards. Standards relevant to requirements development and management: *standards.ieee.org/software/*

- *IEEE STD 1063-1987, IEEE Standard for Software User Documentation*

- *IEEE STD 1362-1998, IEEE Guide for Information Technology — System Definition — Concept of Operations Document*

- *IEEE STD 830-1998, IEEE Recommended Practice for Software Requirements Specifications*

- *IEEE STD P1233/D301998, IEEE Guide for Developing System Requirements Specifications*

Note: The practices recommended in this Memory Jogger™ are aligned with these standards and knowledge area.

SEI

- *www.sei.cmu.edu/*

  The Software Engineering Institute (SEI), established by the U.S. Department of Defense and located at Carnegie Mellon University, has the Capability Maturity Model Integration® (CMMI®). It is a model for helping organizations improve their product and service development, acquisition, and maintenance processes. The CMMI® covers systems engineering and software engineering as well as traditional Capability Maturity

Model® (CMM®) concepts (e.g., process management and project management). The CMMI® includes topics for managing and developing requirements.

- CMMI® for Systems Engineering / Software Engineering Technical Report CMU / SEI-2002-TR-002

Note: Good practices for managing requirements in the CMM® and CMMI® models are included in this Memory Jogger™.

ISO
- *www.iso.ch*

The International Organization for Standardization (ISO) defines standards for the development and implementation of quality management systems in product production and is widely followed by organizations competing in international markets. These standards, like the CMMI®, are not specific to software development practices, but many concepts and guidelines apply to the development process. ISO standards cover the full life cycle of product creation, including identifying customers, documenting and following procedures, monitoring and measuring work, and continuous process improvement.

- ISO / IEC (International Electrotechnical Commission) 12207:1995, *Information Technology — Software Life Cycle Processes*. The 12207 standard has been adapted by the U.S. Department of Defense. (It replaces the military standard MIL-STD-498 and satisfies MIL-Q-9858A (Quality Program Requirements) and ISO 9000 (Quality Systems) for software.) The United States version of the 12207 is IEEE / EIA (Electronic Industries Alliance) 12207:1995.

Note: Good requirements definition and management practices defined in this Memory Jogger™ are aligned with ISO, with an emphasis on internal and external customer satisfaction.

Additional Online Resources

- *www.resg.org.uk*

  The Requirements Engineering Specialist Group of the British Computer Society

- *http://discuss.it.uts.edu.au/mailman/listinfo/re-online*

  Requirements Engineering Online (RE-online) Mailing List

- *web.uccs.edu/adavis/UCCS/reqbib-abcd.htm*

  A comprehensive requirements bibliography

Appendix B: Analysis Models

Focus Question	Goal	Analysis Model To Use	Model Variation You Can Also Use	Goal of Model Variation
Who	Identify people with a stake in the project	Stakeholder categories (Section 3.2)		
	Identify roles that interact with the system	Actor table (Section 4.6)	Actor map (Section 4.6.1)	Illustrate relationships among actors
			Personas (Section 4.6.2)	Describe actors as archetypes (i.e., real people)
			Prototype (Section 4.8.1)	Illustrate examples or mock-ups of the interface
	Illustrate the architecture of the user interface	Dialog maps (Section 4.8)	Dialog hierarchies (Section 4.8.2)	Arrange user dialogs in a hierarchy to show the structure of Web pages
What	Illustrate the functional interfaces in an organization	Relationship map (Section 4.1)		

Continued on next page

Focus Question	Goal	Analysis Model To Use	Model Variation You Can Also Use	Goal of Model Variation
What, cont.	Define the meaning of key business terms	Glossary (Section 2.2)		
	Show the external entities that provide inputs to the system and receive outputs from the system	Context diagram (Section 4.3)		
	Describe entities (groups of data) and their relationships	Data model (Section 4.9)	Class model (Section 4.9.1)	Represent information structures and their behavior for object-oriented technology projects
			Data dictionary (Section 4.9.2)	Describe data groups and their attributes in lists
			Data tables (Section 4.9.3)	Represent entities in tables with sample data

Continued on next page

Focus Question	Goal	Analysis Model To Use	Model Variation You Can Also Use	Goal of Model Variation
When	Identify the events that trigger the system to carry out expected outcomes	Event-response table (Section 4.4)		
	Illustrate the life-cycle changes that data undergoes	State diagrams (Section 4.10)	State-data matrix (Section 4.10.1)	Associate data attributes with states
Why	Define which external and internal standards and regulations must be implemented in software or manual processes	Business policies (Section 4.5)		
	Identify controls that guide behavior and assert the business structure	Business rules (Section 4.11)	Decision tables (Section 4.11.2)	Partition complex business rule components into a matrix

Continued on next page

Software Requirements

Focus Question	Goal	Analysis Model To Use	Model Variation You Can Also Use	Goal of Model Variation
Why, cont.			Decision trees (Section 4.11.3)	Visualize the sequence of conditions evaluated in complex business rules
How	Illustrate the work flow of a business process	Process map (Section 4.2)		
	Describe the tasks performed by the system to fulfill actor goals	Use cases (Section 4.7)	Use case diagram (Section 4.7.1)	Show actors and the use cases they initiate or participate in
			Scenarios (Section 4.7.4)	Describe example actions that occur in response to events (a specific path through a use case)

Continued on next page

Focus Question	Goal	Analysis Model To Use	Model Variation You Can Also Use	Goal of Model Variation
How, cont.			Stories (Section 4.7.5)	Provide a detailed example of actions that occur in response to events from a user's point of view (one or more use case paths)
			Use case maps (Section 4.7.2)	Illustrate dependencies among use cases
			Use case packages (Section 4.7.3)	Show how use cases can be structured into higher level system functions
			Activity diagram of use cases (Section 4.7.6)	Illustrate the flow of complex use cases
			Data flow diagram (Section 4.7.7)	Illustrate inputs, processes, and outputs of a set of related functions or processes in response to events

Appendix C: Verbs and Phrases to Use in Requirements Models

Suggested Verbs for Naming Informative and Performative Use Cases

Note: Use strong action verbs when naming use cases.

Verbs for Informative Use Cases

Access	Find	Query
Analyze	Identify	Request
Answer	Inform	Review
Ask	Investigate	Search
Confirm	List	Select
Consult	Monitor	Show
Determine	Notify	State
Discover	Present	View

Verbs for Performative Use Cases

Achieve	Decide	Extend	Mobilize
Adjust	Decrease	Forecast	Optimize
Allocate	Define	Format	Organize
Allow	Deliver	Grant	Perform
Approve	Design	Implement	Post
Arrange	Develop	Import	Prepare
Assign	Diminish	Incorporate	Produce
Authenticate	Direct	Influence	Promote
Authorize	Distribute	Interpret	Protect
Benchmark	Eliminate	Investigate	Provide
Calculate	Emphasize	Invite	Queue
Calibrate	Enlarge	Invoke	Raise
Change	Enlist	Issue	Recalibrate
Choose	Ensure	Keep	Record
Classify	Enter	Lessen	Refresh
Collaborate	Establish	Lower	Reinforce
Complete	Evaluate	Make	Replenish
Conduct	Expand	Manage	Request
Configure	Expedite	Measure	Resurrect
Coordinate	Export	Merge	Schedule

Continued on next page

Send	Stabilize	Submit	Upgrade
Set up	Stimulate	Sustain	Validate
Specify	Strengthen	Synchronize	

Suggested Verbs and Phrases for Defining Relationship Rules Connecting Entities (in a Data Model)

Accounted for via	Implemented in...carried out
An assembly of...in	Incremented by
An example of	Is a member of
Assigned to	Issued for
Authorized by	Issued to
Based on	Labeled with
Belongs to	Moved via
Bought for	Origin of
Carried out in	Owns
Charged to	Performed on...subjected to
Classified as	Planned for via
Collector of	Prepared by
Comprised of	Provides (coverage, service, product, etc.) for
Created by	Published as
Created to	Reason for
Decremented by	Recipient of
Defined by	Reference to
Defined in	Responsibility for
Delivered as...to fulfill	Responsibility of
Described by	Results in
Described in	Sent via
Destination of	Sold by
Embodied in...an example of	Sought in
Execution of	Source of
Exhibited in	Specified for
Expressed in	Subject to
Generates	Submitted by
Holder of	Taken by
Holds for	
Holds in	

Verbs to Avoid in Relationship Rules

| Associated to | Consists of | Contains |
| Has | Relates to | Uses |

Appendix D: Software Requirements Specification Inspection Checklist

Document Identifier	
Author	
Project Name	
Reviewers' Names	
Inspection Date	

Correctness

❑ Are the requirements stated in a manner that is solution-independent?

❑ Are the requirements free from content and grammatical errors?

❑ Are all internal cross-references to other requirements correct?

❑ Can the requirements be used as the basis for accepting the system?

Clarity

❑ Can each requirement be interpreted in only one way?

❑ Is each requirement uniquely identified?

❑ Are all requirements written at a consistent and appropriate level of detail?

❑ Are the requirements clear enough to be turned over to an independent group for design and implementation and still be understood with minimal explanation?

❑ Are the requirements written concisely (i.e., as short as possible without losing meaning)?

❑ Is each requirement unique and not duplicated by any other requirement?

Continued on next page

Completeness

☐ Are all external hardware and software interfaces defined?

☐ Are all inputs to the system and outputs from the system specified, including their source, accuracy, range of values, and frequency?

☐ Are all of the tasks the user needs to perform specified?

☐ Does each task specify the data used in the task and data resulting from the task?

☐ Are all business rules documented for user tasks?

☐ Is any necessary information missing from a requirement? If so, is it identified as "to be determined (TBD)"?

☐ Are all necessary operational quality attributes (e.g., performance, usability, reliability) specified? Does each precisely state scales of measurement?

☐ Are all necessary deployment quality attributes (e.g., scalability, availability, flexibility) specified? Does each precisely state scales of measurement?

☐ Are all necessary development quality attributes (e.g., testability, efficiency, modifiability) specified? Does each precisely state scales of measurement?

☐ Have important attributes (e.g., status, source owner, release, etc.) been defined for the requirements?

☐ Do the requirements provide an adequate basis for design?

☐ Have the requirements been signed off by the approver and has a formal baseline been created?

Continued on next page

Consistency

❏ Are all requirements in agreement (i.e., devoid of conflict or contradiction)?

❏ Are acceptable trade-offs between competing attributes (e.g., between response time and data currency) specified?

❏ Have the requirements been written in a standard format?

Relevancy

❏ Is each requirement necessary to achieve the product vision?

❏ Have the boundaries, scope, and context for each feature or set of requirements been identified?

❏ Is the implementation priority of each requirement included?

❏ Is each functional requirement necessary to achieve business goals and objectives?

❏ Can each requirement be traced to its origin in the problem environment or to a rationale explaining its purpose?

❏ Are the requirements documented to establish a relationship between each requirement and its sub-sequent design, implementation, and test deliverables?

❏ Can the requirements be used as the basis for accepting the system?

Continued on next page

Feasibility

❏ Is it possible to meet the requirements using existing technologies?

❏ Can the prioritized requirements be met within the approved resources?

❏ Is there at least one design and implementation solution that can correctly implement each requirement?

❏ Can the requirements be implemented within known constraints?

Verifiability

❏ Are the requirements verifiable by testing, demonstration, review, or analysis?

❏ Is each requirement stated in a manner that permits test criteria to be developed and performed to determine if the criteria have been met?

❏ Can the requirements be used to create test plans, procedures, and cases?

Appendix E: Quality Attributes and Metrics

Note: Alternative quality attribute names are listed in parentheses.

Quality Attributes Related to the Operation of the Software

Quality Attribute	Meaning	Possible Metrics
Performance	How well the system performs certain functions. Can be decomposed into speed of response, throughput, storage capacity, and execution time.	Response time after submitting a query; number of concurrent users per period of time, volume of data, screen refresh time, or event-response time
Reliability	The probability of the system executing without failure.	Mean time between repairs; rate of occurrence of failure; probability of failure on demand
Robustness (Fault Tolerance)	The degree to which the system continues to function properly when confronted by failures such as unexpected operation conditions, invalid inputs, or interrupts in hardware or software components.	Time to restart after system failure; percentage of events causing failure; probability of data corruption on failure
Security (Integrity)	The system's ability to resist unauthorized, accidental, or unintended usage while providing access to legitimate users.	Number of attempts or percentage of unsuccessful attempts by type of attempt
Usability	The ease with which the system must be used in a manner that is effective and unobtrusive	Time to get to a specific level of competence to accomplish a specific task for a specific type of user (e.g., "new," "infrequent," or "experienced," each with a clear definition); average number of errors made by users in a given time period; rate of errors by

Continued on next page

Quality Attributes Related to the
Operation of the Software, cont.

Quality Attribute	Meaning	Possible Metrics
		type of user; likeability (as measured by survey reaction); training time needed to complete a specific task; intuitiveness (i.e., probability that a user can complete a specific task without referring to training materials or help facilities)

Quality Attributes Related to the Deployment Environment

Quality Attribute	Meaning	Possible Metrics
Availability	The ability to access the system ("up-time"), considering factors that will affect availability (e.g., backup, recovery, checkpoints, and restart).	Percentage of time available for user access
Flexibility (Extensibility or Adaptability)	Ability of the system to be augmented, extended, or expanded with additional users. Can also mean the ability to build the product incrementally.	Elapse timed, work effort, or cost of adding or modifying specific software components
Interoperability	Ease with which the system can exchange data or services with other systems, including communication protocols, hardware, other software applications, and data compatability layers.	Elapsed time, work effort, or cost for exchanging data or services
Installability	Ability and ease with which the software can be loaded onto the target hardware.	Time to load and configure the software on specific devices
Portability	Ease of moving the software to other machines, operating systems, language versions, compilers, etc.	Cost, work effort, or time to move to a specific target system or environment
Recoverability	Ability to recover the system from failures such as checkpoints, restarts, and backups.	Time to return the system to the state it was in prior to failure

Continued on next page

Quality Attributes Related to the Deployment Environment, cont.

Quality Attribute	Meaning	Possible Metrics
Scalability	Ability to expand the number of users or increase the capabilities of a system without making changes to application software.	Number, range of users to be added, or percentage growth
Safety	Confidence that the system behavior will not harm people or the environment.	Number or percentage of acceptable accidents or harm by type and severity (e.g., human health or property damage); acceptable number of accidents by type and severity; probability of hazard or safety risk by type and severity

Quality Attributes Related to the Development Environment

Quality Attribute	Meaning	Possible Metrics
Efficiency	How well the system utilizes processor capacity, disk space, memory, bandwidth, and other resources.	Percentage of memory, disk space, or processor capability available during certain operations
Maintainability (Modifiability or Supportability)	Ability to correct defects, repair, add new functionality, or perform system support functions. Can also mean the ability to modify the software without taking it out of service.	Time or cost to change or fix specific components of the software
Reusability	Ability to use or convert software components in other systems.	Cost of change required to enable a software component to be integrated within other applications
Testability (Verifiability)	Ease of testing the software components or the entire product for defects.	Cost of demonstrating faults through testing; percentage of defect (by type) by test process, count, or cost of tests to demonstrate defects

Quality attributes in system requirements for complex or critical systems may also include:

- Disposability and toxicity.
- Environmental attributes for the mechanical environment (e.g., dirt and contamination, temperature range, transportation and packaging, and shock and vibration) and the electrical environment (e.g., power supply).
- Labeling.
- Packaging.
- Physical attributes (e.g., weight limits, mechanical construction, physical size and dimensions, color, labeling, and finish).
- Refurbishment.
- Storage and shelf life.
- Transportability (e.g., weight limits and sizes).
- Self-diagnosability.

Appendix F: Ambiguous Words and Phrases to Avoid When Describing Quality Attributes

Ad hoc
Adaptable
Adequate
And/or
Approximately
As a minimum
As applicable
As appropriate
As quickly
  as possible
At least
Automatically
Bad
Be able to
Best practice
Better
But not
  limited to
Came close to
Can
Capability
  of/to
Clearly
Compatible
Completely
Consider
Could
Down to
Easy
Effective
Efficient
Etc.
Excellent
Fast
Fault-tolerant

Flexible
Generally
Good
However
Ideally
If possible
If practical
Intuitive
Large
Least
Lightweight
Like
Low
Many
Maximize
May
Minimal
Minimize
Most/mostly
Nearly
Necessary
Needed
Normal/
  normally
Often
Optimize
Optionally
Portable
Possible
Practical
Provide for
Quality
Quickly
Rapid
Readily

Reasonable
Relevant
Robust
Safely
Same
Seamless
Several
Should
Significant
Simple
So as to
Sometimes
Substantial
Sufficient
Suitable
Support
Target
Timely
To be determined
  (TBD)
Transparent
Typically
User-friendly
Usually
When necessary
Where appropriate
Worse

Appendix G: Questions for Requirements Retrospectives

Setting the Stage

- How well did we define and communicate the product vision?

- How clear was our scope? How might we make it clearer, if necessary?

Stakeholder Involvement and Elicitation

- Did we identify the right stakeholders?

- Were customers involved appropriately?

- How did customers react to the work we did?

- How effective were our requirements elicitation practices?

- Did customers and users understand our requirements documentation?

- Did customers and users believe that we made good use of their time?

Requirements Development and Documentation

- Did we choose the right analysis models?

- How effectively did we verify the analysis models?

- Did we identify the right quality attributes? How well did we quantify them?

- Did we appropriately document requirements?

- Did our requirements documentation follow standard templates? If so, were they effective?

- Did we have enough requirements documentation? Was any portion of the documentation not used or unnecessary?

Software Requirements

- Did developers find our documentation useful as a basis for design, testing, and development?

- Did we adequately define roles and responsibilities? Were roles and responsibilities clear to all team members? Did our team structure and organization work effectively?

- How well did the team communicate during requirements development?

- If there were misunderstandings or failures, why did they happen and how can we make improvements?

Requirements Management

- Have we controlled requirements changes in a timely and appropriate manner?

- How volatile are the requirements and why?

- Did our change control practices help us guard against scope creep?

- Have we captured necessary and sufficient attributes about requirements?

- Did management provide adequate support for our work? If not, what could they have done differently?

Overall Assessment

- What do we want to remember to do again in requirements development or management?

- What surprises or issues have there been?

- What are the top two things we should improve? How?

Appendix H: Glossary

activity diagram: an analysis model that illustrates the flow of complex use cases by showing each use case step along with information flows and concurrent activities. Steps can be superimposed onto horizontal "lanes" for the roles that perform the steps.

actor map: an analysis model that defines the relationships among the actors in an *actor table* in terms of how their roles are shared and disparate. The map shows both human and nonhuman actors arranged in hierarchies.

actor table: an analysis model that defines the roles played by the people and things that will interact directly with the system. At a minimum, the table contains actor names and brief descriptions.

actors: the human and nonhuman roles that interact with the system.

advisor: a person in software development who has relevant information about the product, even if he or she does not directly interact with it.

allocation: see *requirements allocation*.

analyst: a generic name for a role with the responsibilities of developing and managing requirements. Other names include business analyst, business integrator, requirements analyst, requirements engineer, and systems analyst.

baseline: a point-in-time view of requirements that have been reviewed and agreed upon to serve as a basis for further development.

black box tests: tests written without regard to how the software is implemented. These tests show only what the expected input and outputs will be.

business event: a system trigger that is initiated by humans.

Software Requirements

business requirement: a higher level business rationale that, when addressed, will permit the organization to increase revenue, avoid costs, improve service, or meet regulatory requirements.

business rules: policies, guidelines, regulations, and standards that must be adhered to. When defined as analysis models, they are textual statements that define, constrain, or enable the behavior of software or business processes.

cardinality: the number of occurrences of one entity in a data model that are linked to a second entity. Cardinality is shown on a data model with a special notation, number (e.g., 1), or letter (e.g., M for many).

change control board (CCB): a small group of stakeholders who will make decisions regarding the disposition and treatment of changing requirements.

class: system objects with attributes and behavior that often correspond to real-world entities such as people, places, and things.

class model: an analysis model that is conceptually similar to a *data model*, but depicts information groups as classes.

code: a system of programming statements, symbols, and rules used to represent instructions to a computer.

commercial-off-the-shelf (COTS) software: software developed and sold for a particular market.

complex system: a product composed of interrelated parts or subsystems, each with its own operational requirements. Complex system requirements are allocated to software, hardware, or people.

context diagram: an analysis model that illustrates product scope by showing the system in its environment with the external entities (people and systems) that give to and receive from the system.

---

context-free questions: high-level questions about both a product and a process that can be used in requirements interviews as part of requirements elicitation.

critical systems: those systems whose failure can cause significant economic, physical, or human damage to people, organizations, or other entities.

customer: a person who benefits from the product in some way (including the sponsor and product champion).

data dictionary: an analysis model describing the data structures and attributes needed by the system.

data entity: a group of related information to be stored by the system. Entities can be people, roles, places, things, organizations, occurrences in time, concepts, or documents.

data flow diagram (DFD): an analysis model that illustrates processes that occur, along with the flows of data to and from those processes.

data model: an analysis model that depicts the logical structure of data, independent of the data design or data storage mechanisms.

data table: an analysis model that can replace or supplement the data model, showing sets of occurrences in a data entity and sample attributes.

decision tables: an analysis model that specifies complex business rules or logic concisely in an easy-to-read tabular format, specifying all of the possible conditions and actions that need to be accounted for in business rules.

decision tree: an analysis model that provides a graphical alternative to *decision tables* by illustrating conditions and actions in sequence.

defect: see *requirements defect*.

design constraints: software requirements that limit the options available to the system designer.

---

dialog hierarchy: an analysis model that shows user interface dialogs arranged as hierarchies.

dialog map: an analysis model that illustrates the architecture of the system's user interface.

direct user: a person or system that directly interacts with the software. Direct users can be humans who interface with the system, or systems that send or receive data files to or from the system.

elicitation: an activity within requirements development that identifies sources for requirements and then uses elicitation techniques (e.g., interviews, prototypes, facilitated workshops, documentation studies) to gather requirements from those sources.

event-response table: an analysis model in table format that defines the events (i.e., the input stimuli that trigger the system to carry out some function) and their responses.

exploratory prototype: a *prototype* developed to explore or verify requirements.

external interfaces: interfaces with other systems (hardware, software, and human) that a proposed system will interact with.

facilitated workshop: a structured meeting, led by a skilled, neutral facilitator, in which a carefully selected group of stakeholders and content experts work together to define, create, refine, and reach closure on *requirements*.

feature: cohesive bundles of externally visible functionality that should align with business goals and objectives. Each feature is a logically related grouping of functional or nonfunctional requirements described in broad strokes.

focus group: a requirements elicitation technique consisting of group interviews to obtain information from participants.

functional requirements: the product capabilities, or things the product must do for its users.

glossary: a list and definition of the business terms and concepts relevant to the software being built or enhanced.

horizontal prototype: a *prototype* that illustrates a façade of the user interfaces or mimics a shallow portion of the system's functionality.

included use cases: a use case composed of a common set of steps used by multiple use cases.

incremental delivery: creating working software in multiple releases so the entire product is delivered in portions over time.

indirect user: a person who comes in contact with the system's outputs (e.g., files, reports, invoices, and other tangible outputs) or who is affected by system by-products.

inspection: a formal type of *peer review* that utilizes a predefined and documented process, specific participant roles, and the capture of defect and process metrics.

iteration: a process in which a deliverable is progressively elaborated upon. Each iteration is a self-contained "mini-project" in which a set of activities are undertaken, resulting in the development of a subset of project deliverables. For each iteration, the team plans its work, does the work, and checks it for quality and completeness. (Iterations can occur within other iterations as well. For example, an iteration of requirements development would include elicitation, analysis, specification, and validation activities.)

metaquestions: questions about questions that can be incorporated in requirements interviews as part of requirements elicitation. Metaquestions provide feedback to an interviewer and allow him or her to adjust interview questions.

model validation: a technique that traces through requirements models using conceptual tests to detect requirements errors.

---

nonfunctional requirements: the quality attributes, design and implementation constraints, and external interfaces that the product must have.

operational prototype: a *prototype* built to help determine if the system can satisfy user needs.

optionality: defining whether or not a relationship between entities in a data model is mandatory. Optionality is shown on a data model with a special notation.

peer review: a validation technique in which a small group of stakeholders evaluates a portion of a work product to find errors to improve its quality.

problem statement: a brief statement or paragraph that describes the problems in the current state and clarifies what a successful solution will look like.

process map: a business model that shows a business process in terms of the steps and input and output flows across multiple functions, organizations, or job roles.

product champion: a person who ensures that the needs of multiple user communities are met by the product.

prototype: a partial or preliminary version of the system.

provider: a person or party that produces or provides the software product by transforming the requirements into the final product. Providers include analysts, designers, developers, testers, project managers, and software development vendors.

quality attributes: the subset of *nonfunctional requirements* that describes properties of the software's operation, development, and deployment (e.g., performance, security, usability, portability, and testability).

relationship map: a business model that shows the organizational context in terms of the relationships that exist among the organization, external customers, and providers.

---

requirement: the needs that a product must meet to successfully achieve a goal or solve a problem for its users.

requirements allocation: the process of apportioning requirements to subsystems and components (i.e., people, hardware, and software).

requirements defect: an error in requirements caused by incorrect, incomplete, missing, or conflicting requirements.

requirements development: defining the product scope, user requirements, and software requirements by elicitation, analysis, specification, and validation activities.

requirements engineering: a discipline within systems and software engineering that encompasses all of the activities and deliverables associated with defining a product's requirements. Requirements engineering is composed of requirements development and requirements management.

requirements iteration: an *iteration* that results in a subset of requirements. For example, an iteration of requirements would include identifying a part of the overall product scope to focus upon, identifying requirements sources for that portion of the product, analyzing stakeholders and planning how to elicit requirements from them, conducting elicitation techniques, documenting the requirements, and validating the requirements.

requirements management: the activities that control requirements development, including requirements change control, requirements attributes definition, and *requirements traceability*.

requirements management tool: a software tool that stores requirements information in a database, captures requirements attributes and associations, and facilitates requirements reporting.

---

requirements model: a representation of user requirements using text and diagrams. Requirements models can also be called user requirements models or analysis models and can supplement textual requirements specifications.

requirements retrospective: a type of *retrospective* that examines the requirements process to learn how to improve it.

requirements risk mitigation strategy: an analysis of requirements-related risks that ranks risks and identifies actions to avoid or minimize those risks.

requirements trace matrix (RTM): a matrix used to track requirements' relationships. Each column in the matrix provides requirements information and associated project or software development components.

requirements traceability: the ability to identify and document the lineage of each requirement, including its derivation (backward traceability), its allocation (forward traceability), and its relationship to other requirements.

requirements validation: an activity within requirements development that ensures that the stated requirements will meet user's needs. Validation ensures that you built the correct software.

requirements verification: an activity within requirements development that ensures that the requirements satisfy the conditions or specifications of a requirements development activity. Verification ensures that you built the software correctly.

retrospective: a process improvement technique used to learn about and improve on a process or project. A retrospective involves a special meeting in which the team explores what worked, what didn't work, what could be learned from the just-completed iteration, and how to adapt processes and techniques before continuing or starting anew.

risk: a potential adverse occurrence or condition that endangers a project.

scenario: an analysis model that describes a series of actions or tasks that respond to an event. Each scenario is an instance of a *use case*.

secondary actor: an *actor* who participates in but does not initiate a *use case*.

signal event: a system trigger that is initiated by a hardware device.

software requirements: *requirements* for a software product, or the software capabilities of a complex system.

software requirements specification (requirements specification): a requirements document written for the provider audience describing functional and nonfunctional requirements.

sponsor: a person or party who authorizes or legitimizes the product development effort by contracting for or paying for the project.

stakeholder: a group or person who is affected by the product, has an interest in it, or who can influence the project. Stakeholders include sponsors, customers, users, indirect users, providers, advisors, and others, and are therefore sources of requirements.

stakeholder profile: a description of a particular stakeholder's interests, concerns, and success criteria for a product.

state diagram: an analysis model showing the life cycle of a data entity or class.

story: an analysis model, typically documented by users, that describes a path through a *use case*. Stories replace use cases and scenarios in planning releases in iterative software methods.

surrogate (surrogate user): a stand-in or substitute who takes the place of a real user during requirements elicitation.

---

system: a collection of interrelated elements that interact to achieve an objective. System elements can include hardware, software, and people. One system can be a sub-element (or subsystem) of another system.

system requirements: top-level requirements for allocation to subsystems, each of which can be software or a combination of software, hardware, and people.

team review: a type of *peer review* that has some formality (i.e., some roles and phases of more-formal inspections are used).

temporal event: a system trigger that is initiated by time.

timebox: a fixed period of time to accomplish a desired outcome.

traceability: see *requirements traceability*.

Unified Modeling Language (UML): a nonproprietary modeling and specification language used to specify, visualize, and document deliverables for object-oriented software-intensive systems.

use case: an analysis model that describes the tasks that the system will perform for actors and the goals that the system achieves for those actors along the way.

use case map: an analysis model that shows the work flow of a set of use cases.

use case package: an analysis model that illustrates a logical, cohesive group of use cases that represents higher level system functionality.

user: a person, device, or system that directly or indirectly accesses a system.

user acceptance tests: test cases that users employ to judge whether the delivered system is acceptable. Each acceptance test describes a set of system inputs and expected results.

---

user requirement: a *requirement* specifically associated with the user problem to be solved. User requirements are documented from the user's point of view, describing what users need to do with the system and their quality expectations of the system.

user requirements document: a requirements document written for a user audience, describing user requirements and the impact of the anticipated changes on the users.

validation (requirements validation): the stage of software development in which the product is checked to ensure that it satisfies its intended use and conforms to its requirements. Validation ensures that you built the correct software.

verification (requirements verification): the process of checking that a deliverable produced at a given stage of development satisfies the conditions or specifications of the previous stage. Verification ensures that you built the software correctly.

vertical prototype: a *prototype* that dives into the details of the interface, functionality, or both.

vision statement (product vision statement): a brief statement or paragraph that describes the why, what, and who of the desired software product from a business point of view.

walk-through: a type of *peer review* in which participants present, discuss, and step through a work product to find errors. Walk-throughs of requirements documentation are used to verify the correctness of requirements.

Index

abstract testing, 274

acceptance criteria, 270

acceptance tests, 270

activity diagrams, 113, 114, 174-175, 321

actor catalog, 144

actor description, 144

actor hierarchy, 148

actor map, 59, 114, 144, 148-149, 157, 300, 319

actor table, 32, 59, 64, 112, 114, 129, 144-150, 157, 297, 300, 318

adaptation projects, 299

analyst apprentice, 86

analyzing requirements, 109-230

ask why five times, 90

atomic business rules, 211-212

automation lanes, 126

business events, 123, 133, 134, 136, 156, 201

business glossary, 32

business interaction model, 118

business policies, 112, 114, 137-143, 204, 207, 320

business process improvement, 121

business rules, 36, 53, 91, 112, 114, 138, 140, 143, 151, 155, 160, 163, 166, 167, 177, 183, 184, 191, 193, 199, 200, 201, 203, 204-215, 244, 246, 254, 265, 274, 292, 297, 298, 300, 320

cardinality, 188-189, 191, 195

change control board, 285, 287, 289

Notes

Notes